I DANCED WITH MY MOTHER

C.F. SHAPEREL

authorHOUSE®

AuthorHouse™
1663 Liberty Drive
Bloomington, IN 47403
www.authorhouse.com
Phone: 1 (800) 839-8640

Published by AuthorHouse 03/20/2019

ISBN: 978-1-7283-0518-9 (sc)
ISBN: 978-1-7283-0516-5 (hc)
ISBN: 978-1-7283-0517-2 (e)

Library of Congress Control Number: 2019903444

Print information available on the last page.

ACKNOWLEDGEMENTS

There are so many things that keep me inspired. First and foremost, I want to thank my mother for being such an amazing, strong woman and raising me to be the man that I am today. I want to thank my beautiful wife, for being my strongest supporter and having my back through thick and thin. I want to thank all of my children for giving me the fuel I need in order to stay motivated in pursuing my dreams.

I want to thank my siblings for loving me and encouraging me to grow. My father, for raising me to be a great family man such as himself. My grandmothers for loving me, motivating me, supporting me, and encouraging me to follow my dreams, may they rest in peace. My grandfather, who was my best friend and the inspiration for my pen name. He taught me so much about life and how to take on life's obstacles, the good and the bad. He also made sure that I would know how to survive in this world, may he rest in peace.

I also want to thank my entire family for helping me grow, I love you all and I thank you from the bottom of my heart and soul.

This book is a fictional account, any resemblance to real life people, places and things is purely coincidental.

CHAPTER

1

Robbie's life had been a roller coaster with the biggest ups, deepest downs, and curves steep and sharp like the edge of a knife. As a child he had gone through more than most adults encounter in a lifetime. Raised by a single mother of four children, Grace, worked three jobs to care for them all. It was her choice in men though, that had the biggest impact on their lives and their futures. So much of the drama that traumatized them then, still impacts their lives today. The worst of it started when Robbie was four years old. At that very young age, he was the second oldest of the four children, but carried the most responsibility. The family lived in what most people considered the bad part of town otherwise known as the hood. Their dilapidated two-bed room house had holes in the walls, with roaches all over the place, floorboards so rotted that they would creak and crack, crumbling walls, and plastic covering the cracked windows for insulation. There were drug dealers and prostitutes roaming the corners, conducting their own brand of illegal business at all times of the day. Shootings, stabbings, fights, drug busts, and robberies were so much of a daily occurrence that it was something they became accustomed to.

Grace's work schedule required her to have to leave all four children home alone at times. She would try her best to find childcare for them, or friends and family to look after them but the people she found were usually unreliable and all together bad influences. Most of the people Grace would find to care for them would leave home alone, to go out and party. Sometimes the babysitters would invite their friends over to the family home and make the children go to their rooms without eating.

Food was scarce at times, Grace and her children were on welfare, so the cheese, peanut butter, and rice given to them by the government were staples in their daily diet. They would go to the local Department for Family Services to stand in the long lines and carry the boxes of things they were given as they made the long trek home. What made the walks feel even longer was when they occured during extreme weather conditions,

1

walking in the rain, or braving the hot sun for miles resulting in blistered hands and feet.

Grace was a strong and tough woman, so she always gave Robbie and his siblings' tough love. She had also been the oldest of her 3 siblings and she carried most of the responsibility when she was growing up. She was also very close to, her mother, who had kidney issues but would babysit the children occasionally while she worked. One day, during Grace's shift at work, her mother went to sleep, with the oldest two children lying with her, and she never woke up. She had been dead for hours, by the time Grace came home from work. She came into the home to see her two toddlers sitting quietly beside their grandmother's cold body. Grace went into a rage and it changed her forever, it was like she had no emotions, or feelings, like she'd lost the ability to love. She loved her children, she would go on to have two more, but it was like she'd gone numb.

Robbie and his siblings basically grew up in the streets, while Grace worked all day and night they took care of themselves. Robbie was responsible for having the siblings fed and in bed by the time Grace came home. The children barely saw her because she was out running the streets, partying and working. In the midst of the turmoil, Grace routinely dated men who were looking for everything but love. She didn't care though, because she wasn't looking for love either. Until she finally decided to settle down with a man that the children thought would be good for her. Everything was awesome at first, his name was Anthony. Like many men, he started doing what all the right things to get what he wanted. He wined and dined her, made her feel special, he spoiled the children, and they were all so happy that Grace decided to marry him. They didn't realize at the time, but this would be a decision that would impact them all for life.

CHAPTER
2

Shortly after the marriage, things began to change. There was no more wining and dining, no more being nice, or spoiling the children. His whole persona changed, he began to get angry for no reason, started to yell at them, taking away the gifts that he'd bought, and treating the children like they were nothing. Grace was so in love that she wouldn't listen to the children when they tried telling her about the changes in Anthony. He had her mind blown to the point that she would do anything he asked of her. During this time, she also started whipping the children if they did anything that made him angry.

One day Anthony was in their bedroom asleep, resting before he needed to leave for work. He wanted no noise while he was resting so the children either had to stay in their rooms or keep the television volume very low. Robbie knew this about Anthony, but his favorite show, "He-Man" was on and so he turned up the volume and started repeating what his favorite character was saying. Anthony heard him enjoying the show, jumped out of bed, stormed into the room, turned the TV off and told Robbie to come in the room with him. Terrified, he didn't know why Anthony wanted him to come into the bedroom, but he had no choice but to obey his orders. Robbie walked in the room and he was told to close the door. Anthony was sitting at the edge of the bed looking as evil as the devil. He said, "What did I tell you to do when I am sleeping?" Robbie responded, "Be quiet or go to my room." Anthony said, "Why didn't you go in your room?" Robbie said "Because I wanted to watch HE-MAN." Anthony glared and yelled, "Why are you laughing and having a good time, knowing that I have to go to work?" Before Robbie could respond, saying "I wasn't yelling", Anthony slapped him in the face and told him not to lie again. Robbie, down on one knee, was stunned as Anthony took his belt and began to hit him in the back of his head with it as he screamed. Robbie's siblings heard the screams and ran to their rooms to hide. After the beating, Anthony made Robbie kiss his knuckles, blaming him for the small cuts that resulted. He was then sent to his room, hurt and terrified. When his siblings saw him, they all ran to console him. The children were all so mad about what Anthony had done that they plotted to tell Grace when she came home from work.

When Grace arrived, she went straight to her room as she normally did to give Anthony a kiss and take her bath. When she kissed him, he told her that he whipped Robbie for being disrespectful and that she needed to handle him. So, Grace, in rage ran into the children's room turned on the light and told Robbie to get up. She asked why he had been disrespectful, Robbie tried to explain, even showing her his bruises. She responded by telling him not to watch TV again while Anthony was sleeping and made him go back to bed. As Grace walked out Anthony stood there looking at her like she was a fool. Anthony said to her "Baby he disrespected me, knowing I had to go to work, I pay all the damn bills in this house and I demand respect! You need to discipline your child now!" Grace said, "Anthony you already whipped him, I told him that he can't watch television anymore what else do you want me to do baby?" Anthony said, "He need to learn from you because you don't whip him, so you need to beat his ass and teach him that he will respect the king of the castle!" He stood there and looked at her as if he wasn't willing to leave until she did what he said, so Grace begrudgingly whipped Robbie in front of him and as she did this Anthony smiled because he knew he had the power to get her to do anything that he wanted. Grace had a look of remorse and hurt in her eyes because she knew she had betrayed Robbie by turning on him to please a man. As she beat him, she had tears running down her eyes and when she was done she told him to go to bed. The other children stood there and watched in shock and disbelief that she would do such a thing. Robbie felt as if his world was coming to an end. Grace had turned on him for a man, he'd been whipped twice in one day and as she left the room Anthony said, "Baby you did good, he is going to grow up a better man".

CHAPTER
3

Anthony was a very smooth talking and convincing man, he knew how to get Grace to do whatever he wanted her to do by telling her what she wanted to hear and giving her false hopes of love. The sad thing of it all was that, Robbie knew he was manipulating Grace and that he was not who he said he was. But she was so much in love that she was blinded. In her eyes, he was always right, he couldn't do anything wrong, he was her king and she treated him as such. As time progressed things began to get worse by the day. The children went from being independent to feeling like they were living in a prison. Out of the four of them, Robbie was the one who got the worst. Anthony would wait until Grace went to work to start beating him. He always threatened that if the children ever spoke of it to anyone that he would kill them. Robbie wanted to protect his siblings from the beatings because he was the strongest. He knew that when Grace went to work, he needed to be the one that did something to make Anthony mad so that his siblings wouldn't be targeted.

One day it was raining really hard and Grace was running late for work, so she had her youngest son, Jake, take her things to the car to save her time. He took her things to the car, but as he did, he ran through the mud and had gotten it all over his feet. Anthony was in the room pretending to be asleep when Jake came inside out of the rain and tracked mud all over the floor, thinking nothing of it. Grace had left to go to work, and the moment she drove off, as usual Anthony got up and went to the children's room. Anthony said "Who got mud on the floor? Which one of you nasty mother fuckers got mud all over his fucking floor." Robbie knew that if Jake admitted to it, Anthony would have beaten him to the point of no return. And he was too young to handle such a beating. So, Robbie quickly stepped up and said, "Mr. Anthony it was me, I'm sorry it was me!" He knew it wasn't Robbie, because he saw Jake's shoes, so he punched Jake in the chest and told him to go to stand in the corner. He then walked up to Robbie and put his hands around his neck, picking

5

him up and tossing him across the room like a rag doll. As he lay there gasping for air Anthony kicked him in the stomach saying, "Get your ass in his bed room right now, I told you about lying to me nigga!" All of the children started crying, Jake was still standing in the corner hurt and in tears, Anthony had closed his bedroom door so that all they could hear was Robbie being tortured and yelled at. He was in so much pain and terror that he really didn't realize what had just happened. Anthony stood over him and placed his right foot on Robbie's chest, and said "You think you are tough huh?" Robbie responded, "No Sir." He said, "Nigga I know that you didn't track the mud into the house so why did you lie to me" I said, "Because I didn't want you to hurt Jake." He placed his foot and puts it on Robbie's neck, applying pressure to the point that he couldn't breathe and as he started to black out, Anthony released his foot, leaned in and said, "I will kill you if you lie to me again nigga do you understand me." Robbie replied, "Yes sir", and was told to get up and go and get Jake.

Robbie was a protector and there was nothing that he would not do to protect his family. So, he pulled away with angrily and said "No!!!!!! I ain't going to let you hit Jake again!" Shocked and in anger, Anthony said "You are right, I'm not going to beat him, you are!" He headed towards the door, and Robbie jumped on his back. After being thrown off he got back up and went for his leg, biting down as hard as he could. Anthony kicked him in the mouth and busted his lip. Then he grabbed Jake, telling him to pull his pants down while forcing him onto the bed. He handed Robbie a belt and said, "Beat your brother for tracking mud in the fucking house now!" Robbie looked him in the face, blood still dripping from his lip, and said "Mr. Anthony you can beat me all you want to, but you will have to kill me because I am not going to let nobody hurt Jake!" Anthony took the belt, raised Jake up off of the bed, snatched his pants up and put the belt in his hand saying, "Somebody is going to get their ass whipped, so you best better beat your brother's ass right now!" Jake and Robbie looked at each other and Robbie nodded his head to tell him it was ok. Then he pulled his own shorts down and bent over, preparing to be whipped. Anthony said, "Go ahead boy make Robbie pay for your mistake!" Jake started crying and raised the belt, striking him in the back. Robbie nodded his head for him to keep going and he struck him over and over again. Anthony was mad because thought Jake wasn't beating him hard enough, so he snatched the belt away from him, telling him to go to his room. He stood there defiantly and refused to go until Robbie turned around to nod at him to signal for him to go. Only then, did Jake turn around to run out of the room.

Anthony closed the door, turned up the music and beat Robbie so bad that he could hardly walk. When the beating was over, he tried to leave the room but was locked in the closet while Anthony laid down to go to sleep.

CHAPTER
4

While Robbie was locked in the closet he could peep through the crack in the door and see Anthony sleeping peacefully, with no cares in the world. He hated him, and I wished that he was dead. He wanted to break through the door and find anything that he could get his hands on to bash his head in! At such a young age, Robbie had never thought about wanting to kill a human being in so many ways! Sitting in that closet made him think of so much. All he did was think until he fell asleep. As he slept, he heard the door open and Anthony told him to go to his room, saying, in a very calm voice, "Remember what I said boy, remember what I said". When he made it to his room, Robbie passed by to see that his two sisters were sleeping, but Jake had been sitting up all night waiting for him. When Robbie walked in the room he hugged him tight, told him that he loved him and that he hated Anthony. Jake said that he wanted to tell their mother what had happened, but Robbie told him not to tell because she wouldn't listen to them anyway. The children sat and held each other until they fell asleep. Robbie's alarm clock went off 45 minutes after he and Jake had dozed off and it was time for him to get everyone ready for school. He was so stiff and had bruises all over his body, but still managed to get everyone ready for school before Grace came home. Robbie's two sisters knew what was going on but they were too terrified to say anything to anyone. All they did was stare at him with tears in their eyes. Robbie made them wipe their tears before their mother came home and told them to act like nothing was wrong. When Grace got home she came inside of the house and the children except Robbie ran up to her to greet her with hugs and kisses. Seeing the hesitation, she questioned, "Son what is wrong with you?" Robbie responded, "Nothing mama, I just hurt myself when I fell off the bed."

Anthony walked in and greeted Grace, saying "Hey baby, I missed the hell out of you." She asked him how the children had behaved, and he responded, "The kids they were good as usual baby, not a problem in the world." The children all just stared at him in the evilest way when he said that, knowing what he'd done and that he threatened Robbie with death if he told. This became a regular routine for them.

CHAPTER 5

Anthony felt that Robbie deserved to take the punishment for everything that anyone did, even Grace. There were so many times where he just stared at the boy as though he made him sick. He was bothered anytime he would see Grace hug Robbie or show him any kind of positive attention. It was as if he felt threatened by him because Robbie was the one who recognized that he was full of shit. He was using Grace, destroying her mind, luring her in emotionally so that he could do whatever he wanted to do and not worry about her going anywhere. Anthony was a man who had to have control, he wanted to be in charge of everything and everybody, and if he felt like he was losing control or there was something in the way of him gaining power he would do anything necessary to maintain his control. Robbie was very observant and realized about Anthony.

Anthony hated his own mother, he treated her badly and talked to her disrespectfully. He was a pathological liar, had been abandoned by his father, his mother was a drug addict when he was a child and he'd ended up in foster care. He was also a deadbeat dad, and an alcoholic. He had to have a 6 pack of Bull and Mad Dog 20/20 every day. He also smoked like a chimney, bit his nails, was very shaky and seemed as if he had bad nerves. In addition to those qualities, he also had bad hygiene and was always mad at the world. In Anthony's mind, everybody else was always the problem. Robbie didn't see what Grace saw in this sorry excuse of a man, but he was a kid and all he could do was love Grace despite her bad decisions. Robbie never understood why Anthony felt it was ok to do the things that he did. It was like beating him was a drug, so he needed to do it to get his high.

When Robbie made the honor roll which led to his being recognized by the school in the local newspaper, he was so excited to tell Grace. She asked Anthony to go to the store to get a paper, so proud of his accomplishments. But Anthony only pretended to go to the store, and instead stood at the corner smoking a cigarette, returning shortly to tell Grace that the store was out of papers. Robbie was so angry because he knew Anthony hadn't gone to the store at all. He looked at his mom, and said, fearlessly, "Mom he is lying, he didn't go to the store at all, I saw him standing at the corner smoking a cigarette!" Anthony looked at him as if he had lost his mind and said "Nigga you lying! Who the hell are you talking to like that? He then looked at Grace with a very disappointed look at said "Baby I did go to the store you need to check your son! Still angry and with tears running down his eyes, Robbie said "I'm talking to you!" Grace quickly said, "Boy shut up, don't you talk to no grown-ups like that!" But he was to the point that he was fed up and I didn't care if Anthony decided to kill him. This was his time that he'd worked so hard for and he was not willing to let his moment be ruined. Grace, confused and trying to figure out who was lying, laid her hand on his head, looked him in the eyes and said, "Son go to your room until I can see what's going on." Determined, Robbie responded "Mom please believe me, just let me go to the store myself and get the newspaper please." Anthony turned around and stormed off to their room, slamming the door behind him. Grace gave Robbie 50 cents and told him to go to the store.

He ran to the store as fast as he could, and as he ran, there was the strangest feeling that someone was watching him. When he turned to look back, he noticed Anthony sanding at the window, looking as if he wanted to kill him. Robbie knew he had to prepare himself for the worst, but he was ready to go through whatever he had to go through. He went inside the store and said, "Hey Mr. Clark do you have any newspapers left, I made the honor roll and my name is in it." Now, Mr. Clark, was a cool guy who had a crush on Grace. He always flirted with her when she came to the store and he had this thing called store credit that he did with Grace. Store credit was when you didn't have money to buy anything and Mr. Clark would allow you a certain balance of credit that you could use to go get whatever you wanted but you had to pay the balance by the end of the month. He knew about Anthony and Grace being married, but he didn't like it. He always told Grace that she made a mistake with that man, but she was too blind to see. When Robbie told him about his accomplishment he was very happy and congratulated him! Mr. Clark always encouraged Robbie to stay in school and in the books because he said one day would be somebody. After opening the paper and finding Robbie's name Mr. Clark said, "Well I'll be damned congratulations little buddy, I will give you 3 papers and get anything that you want out of the store, on me!" Robbie was so excited that he went to get his favorite candy cow tails, caramel candy, a mountain dew and for Grace, a honey bun and Pepsi cola. He even grabbed a couple of treats for his siblings and went back to the front of the store, saying "Thank you so much Mr. Clark! Anthony told my mom that he came in here and there were no papers."

Mr. Clark said, "Son that punk didn't come in here not one time today, why would he do such a thing?" Robbie wanted to tell him what was happening, but he had always been taught to not tell strangers their family business, so he responded, "I don't know Mr. Clark, I just don't know." Mr. Clark said, "Son, please be careful around that man, there is something about him that isn't right, I tried to tell your mother, but I don't have a clue why she didn't listen to me. You take care of her. Ok?" It was so hard for Robbie to keep it together, but he I did and responded, "Yes Sir! Thank you so much!" Mr. Clark shook his hand and patted him on the back, sending him on his way.

Robbie always loved walking to the store because it was a chance to get away from the hell hole and Anthony. He also used that time to plot about things that he could do to get Anthony to vanish from their lives forever. He had so many things running through his head, thinking about what Mr. Clark said, he knew that he had to take care of Grace and protect his siblings from Satan himself. With every step he took, he had a different thought of what he could do to him. He had ideas like putting bleach in his food, hitting him in the head with a hammer while he was asleep, going to school and report him to the teachers, telling one of the drug dealers about him and asking them to kill him, stabbing him in the throat while he was slept, poison, etc. There was so many ideas that crossed his mind that day, and to Robbie, all of them made sense, but he was too nervous to try any of it. He didn't want anything to go wrong which could lead to things backfiring and getting worse. Robbie loved to sing, and his favorite song was "I Won't Complain" so every time that he walked to the store he would sing it because his grandmother had told him to do so any time he felt that he needed God. As he got closer to home, he saw Anthony standing in the yard talking to one of his friends. So, he went around to the back of the house, so he wouldn't be noticed.

Grace was standing in the kitchen cooking fried chicken and mashed potatoes. When Robbie made it inside, she looked at the bag he was carrying and said, "Boy where did you get all of this stuff from?" Robbie responded, "Mr. Clark told me to get whatever I wanted for making the honor roll, and he said that Anthony never came in the store to get a paper." Looking confused and angry, Grace was in disbelief that Anthony would lie to her about going to get the paper. Robbie wanted to tell her so bad that he had done that because he didn't like him, but he knew that it would cause a major argument and things would go bad. So, Robbie just responded that he didn't know why and she told him that she would discuss it with Anthony when he came back in. When she saw the article about Robbie, she got very emotional and began to cry. Hugging Robbie, she said "Son I am so proud of you, mama may not have been the smartest thing, but her kids are!"

CHAPTER 6

Grace never really thought she was good enough or smart enough. She always put herself down but to Robbie, she was the best mother in the world. He never saw her as unintelligent or not good enough. She may have not been perfect but there was nothing that you could tell him that was bad about Grace. And she always taught her children street knowledge and common sense. She was also smart in other ways besides books, she was a hustler and knew how to get what she wanted, when she wanted it, no questions asked. She was a sucker for the wrong kind of love, but it was mostly due to her own upbringing. Her father was never around so she was pretty much raised by her grandmother who worked 3 jobs and was also a hustler. Grace had been through so much as a child that it was unbelievable. She'd been raped, homeless, there were many stories about her fighting, selling drugs, and getting pregnant at a very young age. All of this led to her giving her children tough love. She was scarred by her past. Being abused mentally and physically throughout her childhood is what caused her to live the way she did.

Grace had eyes that stared right through your soul, her eyes told you everything that she was thinking, and they also told you that she was reading everything that you were thinking and had already thought. Her eyes were so powerful and demanding but yet loving and calming. Robbie just adored Grace and wanted to be like her in many ways. He understood that the violence that shaped her childhood was also his, like a generational curse.

If felt so good for Robbie to hear Grace say that she was proud of him, it wouldn't have mattered if the President had told him that, the only person that mattered to him was Grace. He always wanted to make her happy, joyful, and he loved to see her smile. Life always felt so good to Robbie when it was he, his mother, and his siblings. He cherished every opportunity that they had to be away from Anthony, and all of the happiness they felt would soon turn into sadness. Anthony stayed gone for a while and moments like this was like heaven. Robbie wanted him gone and had prayed to God to take him out of their family. Even Grace could tell the difference, the calmness in atmosphere when Anthony was not around. This feeling was always seemed too good to be true and it was because just as they were having real family time, watching TV, cuddling with Grace, Anthony came back into the house. He stood in the door way and gave them the evilest look, like he was disgusted, Grace said to Anthony, "Robbie's name was in the paper that he got from Clark's. Where you told me, they had no papers left…we need to talk later ok!" Anthony looked at her, nodded his head, winked at Robbie, and stormed to his room, slamming the door behind him.

Robbie knew that wink meant, Grace had to go to work and he would deal with him when then. He had to get his mind right and prepare himself for the beating that was coming. His siblings were afraid for him. His baby sister, Tori stared at him with tears in her eyes and Grace looked at her, asking what was wrong. Before she could respond, Robbie spoke up saying, "Mama, she's probably just sleepy. She's been yawning all day." Grace asked her if she was sleepy, and Tori looked at Robbie, then back at their mother, nodding her head in agreement. It had gotten late and, the children had school the next day. Grace told them to get ready for bed and that they had to get themselves ready for school the next day because she wouldn't be there in the morning, she had to go to court. Robbie thought to himself, about being there alone with Anthony, deciding that he needed to figure out a plan. As he lay in bed, all kinds of thoughts were going through his head about what Anthony would do to him. He was so anxious about it all that he said a prayer to God for protection. Despite this, in his heart, he I had little faith in God because he had been praying for protection from Anthony and it hadn't happened yet. Their alarm would go off at 5:45, every morning. Robbie was like a father to his sisters and brother, getting them ready and walking them to school every day. Anthony would get up every morning by 6:30 am so he figured that if he had set the alarm to 5:30 am that the children all could get dressed and be gone before he woke up. He knew that Anthony was ready to make him pay for what had taken place that day.

That night, Robbie dreamt, he and Grace was listening to music in a jail cell, but they were both happy. They were all laughing and having a grand ole time, it was the happiest that he had even seen her. They felt so free and it was just the two of them. She grabbed his hand and they danced. The music had them getting down, then suddenly the music stopped, and it got really dark, Anthony was standing there and all you can see were his eyes, demonic and evil looking. He lunged forward, lifting Grace up and throwing her down, causing her to hit her head on the floor. Then he came for Robbie, but Grace wouldn't let Anthony get to him. She pulled his leg and he kicked her. Robbie screamed, trying to get him off Grace and suddenly Anthony vanished, and Robbie woke up. He didn't understand the meaning of the dream or why he had it, but it felt too real.

He woke up at 5:25am but when he sat up in bed, his heart dropped because Anthony was standing there in the doorway watching him. Robbie was so scared that he peed in his clothes, he didn't know what to do. He fully expected to get the beating of his life but was too scared to move. Robbie had thought he'd outsmarted him, but he had been outsmarted by Anthony who had made it his business to be standing there when he woke up. It was like he knew what Robbie was thinking before he thought it, he knew this kid's every move and there was nothing that he could do about it. The other children were still asleep, so he pointed at Robbie, motioning for him to come with him. Robbie slowly followed as he led him to the back door. He stared at him confused because the beatings usually occurred in the bedroom. He wondered why Anthony was leading him out the back door and into the back yard. It was raining outside, and Anthony wore a long rain coat but motioned for Robbie to come outside dressed as he was, in his night clothes. He didn't want to do that, he was tired and fed up with being treated this way and decided that he was not going down without a fight. Robbie stood in the door way defiantly, saying "No! I am not going out there in the rain!" He turned to run away, but Anthony grabbed ahold of him and threw him outside in the mud. Robbie was so angry that he no longer cared if Anthony tried to kill him. He tried to fight, kicking and punching at him but Robbie's strength was no match for that of a grown man. He slapped Robbie and told him to shut up or he would do it again saying, "Nigga I got 15 minutes to show you what death is like!" He put Robbie's face in the mud and said, "When a king tells his servant to do something and they disobey him they pay!"

While Robbie lay in the mud, Anthony pressed his foot into the center of his back, telling him to never snitch on him again. The longer it took for Robbie to respond to this command, the more pressure Anthony applied to his back. Robbie was too weak to do anything, so he put his face in the mud and rain water, hoping to drown. He wanted to die right then and there because he was so tired of being treated this way, so he figured that if he died, Anthony would go to jail and his family would be ok. He kept applying pressure to Robbie's back as he lay face down in mud saying, "I told you that I would kill you, I told you that you would never disrespect me!" when there was no response to his taunts, he snatched Robbie up and saw that he was barely breathing, and nearly drowned, so he laid him on his back and performed CPR on him.

Barely conscious, Robbie had a vision of himself in a blank space standing with Grace, she was so happy and beautiful, and the children were smiling, having a great time. Then the blank space turned into a bad storm and he was running to get Grace's hand, but Anthony was pulling him to prevent him from reaching her. When Robbie turned to pull away from him, he felt himself being snatched up and woke up spitting out water, looking right into the face of the devil! He sat Robbie up and told him to get in the house to get ready for school. He was dazed and didn't know what had happened. Robbie walked to his room slowly to get ready for school but was still not feeling like himself. He woke his siblings up to get them ready and fed as they all looked at him strangely. Robbie's older sister, Lana said, "What happened? What did he do to you, tell me!" Still in a daze, he simply responded "Nothing."

That day at school, everyone who had made the honor roll got ice cream at the end of the day, but after the experience that Robbie had at home, he didn't want anything to do with the honor roll. Anthony was getting to him, breaking him down, and he was winning. Robbie was a small child, dealing with adult stress, he just wanted to give up and die. He thought that if he let Anthony kill him, his mother and siblings would finally be free because he would go to prison for life. Death began to sound better and better. Robbie reasoned that his mom probably wouldn't date for a while which would give her time to get herself together and really focus on the children. And finally, the suffering would end. The more he thought about it the closer he was to deciding to do something that would provoke Anthony into hurting him so badly that it would kill him. He planned it all out, at 6 years old, a plan to facilitate his death. Robbie's plan was to start disrespecting Anthony really bad, turning up the TV while he was sleeping, acting happy, as if he didn't like him, care about him or fear him. Or he'd just talk back to him so that he'd be angry enough to beat him to death. But before that, Robbie would write a letter apologizing to his family, assuring them that his death was what was best for them. All he wanted was for his family to be happy and he was willing to give his life to protect them.

As these thoughts filled his mind, he began to have doubts and started second guessing himself. Even if Anthony was out of Grace's life, she would be without Robbie and that would hurt her. Also, his siblings really needed him, because he was their strength, he protected them, took care of them and they loved him so much. Suddenly Robbie felt that his death might do more harm than good, and he didn't want to make the wrong decision. So, he asked God to help him and his family, and to also give him a reason to want to live. He still believed that one day God would answer, but until then, he would have to put up with the abuse. Robbie kept so much inside, that Grace would never have imagined the state of mind he was in.

CHAPTER
7

Every year, Grace would bring her children to the annual Family Reunion. Anthony never went along because he knew that no one there liked him. Many members of Grace's extended family thought he was just using her for what he could get. This time though, he decided to go to the reunion with them. Grace seemed to have mixed feelings because she knew her family disliked Anthony, but she was the type of woman that stood by her man no matter what, so she was excited that he wanted to go. Robbie was actually happy that he was going because he hoped that something would happen to cause his family members to confront Anthony. Robbie was ready to sit back and enjoy the show.

As the children got into the car, Grace lifted up the seat so that they could get in the back. Anthony suggested that Robbie get into the car on his side because he would be able to adjust the seat, as the lever on Grace's side of the seat no longer worked. So, Grace advised Robbie to go to his side, and as he got into the car, Anthony thumped him on the back of his head and forced him into the back seat. Then he deliberately slid the seat so far back that Robbie's legs were pressed uncomfortably and began to hurt. When Robbie tried to bring this to his attention, he reached back and pinched the side of his leg, which meant 'shut up and deal with it'. As the family rode along in the car, Anthony stared at Grace and she looked back at him and said, "What baby? What is it?" he looked at the children and back at her responding, "Nothing baby I am just so happy to have such a beautiful family, I know the children have their moments, but I love you and I love the kids! I always dreamed of this and I have it now, thank you baby."

All four children were so disgusted that they wanted to throw up, all looking at each other, slowly shaking their heads. Grace was a softy for her man, and responded to him, with happy tears in her eyes, "Aww, baby that was so sweet of you, we thank God for you and the children love you too, isn't that right kids?" Everyone got quiet and no one responded to Grace's comment, so she repeated her question, "Isn't that right kids?" Everyone slowly nodded their heads as if they were saying yes except Robbie who pretended to be asleep, but he could see Anthony watching him in the rear-view mirror. He refused to ever utter that phrase, Robbie didn't love him and never would.

It was a very long and quiet drive. Robbie eventually noticed Grace watching him in the rear-view mirror, she knew that he wasn't sleep, and she knew that none of them loved Anthony. But she was a woman who had always wanted a complete family, and a man that would love her kids as much as he loved her. She suspected that there was more going on with Robbie and Anthony, as she stared at each of them, trying to read their faces. In Robbie's mind, Grace deserved to be happy, she was amazing, and gorgeous, she did not deserve a low life like Anthony. And deep down she knew it too but like so many other times in her life, she was trying to find the good in a seemingly hopeless situation.

As the family pulled up to the Reunion, Grace gave them the speech, typical of most parents, telling them to act like they had some sense and to not act up. Then Anthony, trying to insert his input…added, "Don't be embarrassing us because me and your mama didn't raise ya'll to act up and you will get your butts whopped." Everyone said "yes sir" but Robbie, so Anthony told Grace to go ahead that he was coming because he needed to talk to Robbie and that they would catch up. Robbie looked at his mom, pleadingly so she wouldn't leave him, but she left anyway. Once Grace and his siblings walked away, Anthony turned around in the seat saying, "What the fuck is your problem you little bitch ass nigga?" Robbie's only response was a cold stare. Then he grabbed Robbie by his shirt saying, "You want to try me boy, I don't give a fuck about your little punk ass family I will beat your ass right in front of them, you better respect me do you hear me?" Robbie still said nothing, so he punched him in the shoulder and told him to get out the car, threatening to deal with him later. Robbie fixed his shirt as he walked away, turning to glare at him angrily and headed into the family reunion.

He was greeted with lots of hugs, making him feel so special in spite of the bullying and intimidation he'd just been subjected to by his stepfather, Anthony. Grace looked at his eyes, as if she knew that something had happened, asking where Anthony was. Robbie simply pointed outside, and a look of disappointment came across her face because he still hadn't come in to socialize with the family. People were asking her where he was and why was still outside. Robbie didn't care if he came in, but he did want the family to confront him because he needed to be put in his place. While Grace was headed to find Anthony, Robbie decided to enjoy spending time with his extended family. He was very mature for his age, so Robbie hung around the older people in the family and they loved him so much. The music was playing, he was dancing and enjoying himself, entertaining the family like always but he started to worry because Grace hadn't come back inside. He decided to go outside to check on her and as he got closer to the door, he heard yelling. Anthony and Grace were arguing because he was outside smoking and drinking instead of coming inside to hang out with the family. This man was rude, and something had to be done about it because he was cursing at Grace and Robbie didn't like it, but he was in the right place to get some help.

Robbie ran back inside and told his cousins that his mom was outside with Anthony and for them to please go and check on her. As soon as they were ready to walk outside, Grace and Anthony came in, smiling as if nothing had happened. This frustrated Robbie big time! He was hoping that the cousins would find his mom and Anthony arguing then beat him up, but the plan didn't work. Anthony walked in shaking everyone's hands, hugging them like he was the best person in the world, trying to win Grace's family over. He was putting on the biggest front, so convincing and manipulative that he was fooling the family into thinking that he was a good person even though they had heard so may bad things about him. Anthony danced, played cards, everything that he could to win the family over. So, Robbie thought to himself about what he could do, and the first thing that came to his mind was to give his mom a hug, a kiss on the cheek and ask to her to dance with him.

Grace was sitting down with the family, having a great time because family was very important to her, it was the one thing that made her truly happy. Anthony had been playing cards and drinking so Robbie felt it was the perfect time to put his plan into play. He walked up to his mom, gave her a hug and kiss telling her that he loved her. Anthony watched and his whole mood changed. The family members were all commenting about how sweet Robbie was and that he was "such a good child". Anthony smiled and said to Grace, "Baby, can I have a kiss too?" But Robbie immediately asked Grace to dance with him, there was good music playing, his mom loved to dance, and she was a really good dancer. His request caused her to ignore Anthony's, and she came out to the dance floor with Robbie to have a good time. Their family members were cheering them as they danced happily to the music. Robbie knew that his plan was working because Anthony got up angrily and walked outside to smoke a cigarette.

He was so mad that he wanted to kill Robbie. When they were finished dancing, Grace noticed that Anthony was gone and asked me where he was. He'd gone outside, something he'd done to purposely get Grace's attention. He wanted her to chase after him, catering to his feelings and needs. One thing about Grace though, was once she was around her family and was having a good time, she wasn't going to stop. Which meant "To hell with Anthony and his feelings", she went back on the dance floor and they started a soul train line. This made Anthony so upset that he stormed in and asked Grace if he could he talk to her, Grace told him that when she was finished dancing she would talk to him. Meanwhile, Robbie was pulling Grace to dance with him, going down the soul train line as Anthony made his requests, and she'd turned away from him.

Anthony responded by flying into a rage and in front of the whole family snatched her hand and said, "What did I say, you need to come talk to me right now dammit!" Robbie's plan had worked and because Grace's male cousins didn't play about someone putting their hands on anyone in the family. Suddenly, the music stopped and five of Grace's cousins got up, standing inches from Anthony's face, asking what the hell his problem was. All of the children at the reunion were then told to go outside, because things were getting serious. Robbie decided to hide behind a speaker and stay inside to listen to what was happening. Grace was hurt and embarrassed that Anthony had done that in front of the family. There were two of her cousins blocking the door and three standing in his face waiting to get to the bottom of this temper tantrum that he had thrown. Anthony then looked at the men standing around menacingly and asked them if he could just have a talk with Grace, he apologized for what he had done. But it was too late, the cousins weren't going anywhere, no matter what Grace told them to do. They told Anthony that he can say whatever he needed to say in front of them, so Grace told him to talk. Anthony looked around and then looked at Grace saying, "I was asking you to give me a kiss and you ignored me because of that mama's boy asking you to dance. All you had to do was give me a kiss and I would've been fine, but you just totally ignored me." Grace was very upset and responded, "Nigga, that's my son, this is my family reunion and you have the nerve to disrespect me in front of them. Don't no damn body put their hands on me Anthony what has gotten in you! Do you not like my son? Because I am sick of you acting like he is a problem!" Anthony, breathing hard, fast and angrily said "I told you I apologized, and I don't appreciate you trying to jump in my shit in front of your family, I am your husband. I am your king I come first, and your son needs to understand that because I raise him I keep them when you go to work, and I deserve respect! Yes, he is a mama's boy with his spoiled ass he needs his ass whopped being in grown folks business!" Grace snapped and told Anthony that he needed to leave, she had nothing to say to him. The family members quickly escorted him out of the building and told him to call a cab. He looked at Grace and told her that he will see her when she gets home, and he gave her a look that implied that this wasn't over.

Robbie was feeling pretty good about himself, his plan was a success, or so he thought. The family told Grace that she needed to get rid of that man because "he seemed crazy in the head", they said that "something wasn't right about him at all" and told her to be careful especially with the kids alone with him. For the first time in his life Robbie thought that Grace had finally listened. The family reunion continued, but Grace seemed a bothered even though she tried to block out what had gone on with Anthony. At the end of the reunion they all took a family picture and loaded up the car to head home. The happiness level went from 100 to 0 really quick when Robbie realized that his plan may have backfired. He began to worry that when the children got home Anthony would blow up. As the children drove home Grace said to them, "Kids, I am sorry for all of the mistakes that I have made trying to raise ya'll. Mama is not perfect. I only want what's best for ya'll. I want you to know this ok." The children all said yes ma'am and that it was ok. She acted like she regretted the decision that she had made to marry Anthony. She knew that now that he was in their life, it was going to be hell getting him out. But during the ride home they focused on enjoying their time together. The car ride was happy and peaceful the children laughed, sang songs and had fun. Before they pulled up to the house, Grace had already told the children to go straight to their rooms, take a bath and get dressed for bed. She instructed them all not to say anything to Anthony, no matter what. All while Robbie worried about what was coming next. He had already started to blame himself for what may be about to happen.

When they pulled up to the house all of the lights were off, they walked inside to do exactly as Grace had instructed. To their surprise, Anthony was not home, and they didn't know whether to take that as good or bad news. Robbie was already thinking of all sorts of possible outcomes, one being the thought of Anthony coming home to kill them all. Grace tried to ease Robbie's mind, telling him to go to bed and that she would be ok. But he decided to stay awake, watching and listening the entire night, periodically getting up to check on Grace, and Anthony never showed up. When Robbie finally went to sleep, it was nearly morning. There was no school the next day, so the family was able to sleep in a little later than usual. When Robbie did wake up, he smelled breakfast being cooked was so excited and happy. Grace was the best cook in the world to her children. He got himself dressed and raced to the kitchen to greet her. "Good Morning Son" Grace said as she grinned, and Robbie hugged her tight. Anthony was not home, Robbie was happy but shocked that he had not been home all night. Grace seemed to not have a care in the world but Robbie, ever the worried child, knew it all felt too good to be true.

CHAPTER
8

Watching Grace prepare meals for the family was one of Robbie's favorite pastimes. He always wanted to learn because she'd always told him that one day he would need to know how to cook for himself. As he sat intently, watching Grace prepare her famous country breakfast, there was a knock at the front door. She sent Robbie to see who was knocking, and he tried to prepare himself mentally in case it was Anthony, but he recognized that it was one of Anthony's friends. He had stopped by to let Grace know that Anthony had been walking on the side of the road from the family reunion when he was hit by a car, which resulted in him being transported to the hospital. In a panic, Grace stopped cooking breakfast and told the children to hurry to get dressed so that they could head to the hospital.

Robbie was smiling on the inside, wishing and hoping that Anthony was dead. He hated everything about him and in his mind, Anthony deserved what had happened to him, and then some. Grace, on the other hand, was devastated. She was crying, shaking, and blaming herself for what happened to him. She kept saying that if she would not have told him to leave that he would not have left walking and would have ended up in the hospital. All along, if she had known what Anthony had been doing to her children, she would have wished death on him as well. Grace cried the whole way to the hospital so Robbie knew that Anthony was about to be back on her good side. He wondered if Anthony had intentionally gotten himself hit by a car just to make Grace feel guilty. He was certainly capable of doing anything to get his way, including self-harm and manipulation. Grace and the children rushed through the hospital doors, she hurriedly got Anthony's room number from the receptionist and as they rode the elevator up, she began whispering to herself, "Lord what have I done, what have I done".

When they made it to his room, Anthony was lying in the hospital bed with one leg up watching television and laughing. But the moment he saw Grace he went into baby mode. She went to sit down on his bed and he acted as if he was terribly injured. She hugged him and expressed how and how bad she had felt about him being hurt. Anthony looked at her and responded, "It's ok baby, I forgive you. People make mistakes all of the time, couples fight and make bad decisions, but they make up for it. I love you baby and I am so glad that you and the kids are here." Robbie was sick to his stomach, knowing that this was all an act, but it had gotten the best of Grace. As she hugged him and cried, he looked at Robbie, winked and then frowned.

Anthony went into great detail describing how he had almost been killed and left for dead by the person who ran him over. And to make Grace feel even worse, he said, "When we got into that argument at the family reunion, I was really hurt I felt alone like I had lost my best friend. I felt like you had turned on me and I just wanted to disappear, I wanted to die because I know that I hurt you too. So instead of calling a cab I took off walking and I was in tears. As I was coming around that curb by the school there was this car that came flying around and hit me and knocked me into the tree. I thought that the person was going to stop but they kept going and I had nobody to call I was in the middle of nowhere. You had kicked me to the curb and everybody hated me so luckily a police officer came and saw me and called the ambulance. I am not hurt too bad; my leg is bruised and I have a few scratches I guess I was lucky baby." Robbie rolled his eyes in disgust. He was barely hurt and was sitting there as big as he was, acting like a little baby. Anthony's strategy worked, and all Robbie could do was prepare himself for what was about to happen. The next day, Anthony was discharged from the hospital. Once he was back home, laying on the couch with his feet up putting on the biggest front in the world, Robbie stared at him from his room with the look of deep hatred. Grace took off from work for two full weeks, using up all of her vacation days, just to take care of Anthony.

During his recovery time, Anthony acted so innocent, he acted like he loved them all, and acted as if Grace and the children were the best thing to ever happen to him. He wanted them all to watch TV together, play monopoly, when it rained he wanted to tell them ghost stories, he acted very affectionate, he tried to hug all of them and play with them, but Robbie was the only one that stayed away from him. He played the role so good that he even had Robbie's siblings fooled, despite the fact that they knew the terrible things Anthony had done to him. Robbie knew that Grace would be going back to work soon and that he would be back to being the abusive psycho he truly was. Robbie found himself feeling upset with his siblings about their newfound loyalty to Anthony. They made peace with the enemy and had fallen for his trickery. He was so good at manipulating them that they started calling him "Dad". All the times Anthony had locked Robbie in the closet, starved, beat and treated him like a slave, and his siblings still defended him. Robbie felt as if nobody was on his side, so he had to come up with a plan that would end this once and for all.

The time did come when Grace had to go back to work, it was a Monday night she had started a new job as a maid at a hotel. All Robbie could think was that this was the worst thing that could have happened because it meant that his mom would be gone more during the night. That night, she came in their rooms and told them all to be good and not to make a lot of noise so that they wouldn't bother Anthony. He responded, "Baby they are going to be just fine, we have respectful kids and they listen very well." The children all gave her hugs and kisses as he stood at the door watching patiently with the weirdest smirk on his face like he was up to something. Then he walked up behind Grace and hugged them all like they were one big happy family. During the hug though, he gripped Robbie's shoulder so hard that he pulled away. It was then that he knew for sure that he would be in for a rough night.

After Grace left for work, the children turned off the lights and tried to get to sleep. Everyone went to sleep quickly except for Robbie because he was ready to deal with the madness that he knew was coming his way. Hours went by and nothing happened, Robbie heard him laughing at the television, but he made no movement towards the bedroom. Then all of a sudden there was a light knock on the door, and Robbie heard him walk towards the room to see if the children were sleeping so he closed his eyes tightly to pretend to be asleep. Anthony stood there for 2 to 3 min and then he walked away. Next, he went to the door and let someone in, and was whispering to the person as they both went into Grace's room. As soon as Robbie heard the door close, he quietly got up and tip-toed to the room to see who this could be coming into Grace's house at this time of night. And he knew it wasn't his mother. After putting his ear to the door, he heard a woman's voice that sounded very familiar. Anthony asked her why didn't she wear the red ones because she knows what he likes and she replied "Baby you know there's plenty more where that came from now stop your whining and make love to me big daddy."

Robbie was devastated, as he heard Anthony having sex with another woman in his mother's home while she worked so hard to take care of all of them. Tears rolled down his eyes because he was telling her that he loved her and how she felt better than Grace and that Grace didn't do it like she did it. Robbie stayed at the door the entire time and heard him tell this woman how stupid Grace was, how he was going to keep using her, how he hated them all and that he was going to leave Grace soon and to just give him some time!

After things got quiet, Robbie went back to his room to pretend to be asleep, and Anthony quietly walked to their rooms to check on them. He had no clothes on, and she was fully dressed behind him. Robbie saw the woman's face out the corner of his eye and immediately recognized her as his mother's best friend, Charla. His heart dropped because they had known this lady since they were babies, she had been a friend of the family and like a sister to Grace. When she left, Anthony went into the bathroom and took a shower.

Robbie had fallen asleep and jumped up, startled when his alarm went off. It was then that he realized that Anthony hadn't tried to come back to torture him in the night. He got up to get himself and his siblings ready and headed to the kitchen to fix them all a bowl a cereal. As he walked by Grace's room he heard Anthony snoring like a bear that had been hibernating for winter. As Robbie fixed bowls of cereal for his siblings, his older sister, Laura came and put her hand on his shoulder and said, "If you do it mommy will be mad at you." Robbie responded angrily, "What are you talking about? Leave me alone I don't care!" She said, "Kill him, I won't tell anybody but if you do it mommy will be mad at you and she will not love you anymore." Robbie said, "How do you know that I want to do that, stop making stuff up you don't know what you are talking about!" She said, "I know because I want to kill him too brother! I hate him a lot and I don't want him to live anymore!"

Robbie had been really angry with her and because of how, before, she'd taken his side and called him daddy, so he said "You make me sick because you took his side and you called him your daddy so stop trying to set me up, so you can run and go tell mommy! I don't want to kill him at all, so you don't know what you are talking about!" Laura glared at Robbie, shoved him out of her way and sat down to eat her cereal.

Soon after, the children heard Grace's car pull up and they all went to their rooms to get their book bags. Grace walked in and smiled at Anthony as he slept like he was the best thing that ever happened to her. Robbie wanted to tell her that Anthony and Charla had been in her room having sex, talking about them and saying that he was using her. But he knew that he she would probably think he was making it up. All of the children came running and yelling "Mommy!! Mommy!!!!" This woke Anthony up, and she told them to be quiet, but it was too late. He came out as if nothing had ever happened and said, "Baby where have you been all my life I missed you girl!" Grace embraced him tightly and said, "I been right here daddy" she kissed him and asked him how everything had gone last night. He looked her in her eyes and told the biggest lie ever, saying, "Everything was great baby, I watched TV, read the bible and dozed off with your picture right beside me!"

Robbie was so mad that he walked away, angrily bumping into his sisters and brother which made Grace call him to come back, saying "Boy, get your little ass over here right now and I mean now dammit!" He slowly walked up to her and she snatched him to her saying, "What is your problem? Do you have a problem because I can fix it for you right now?"

29

He looked at her with tears running from his eyes and responded, "No ma'am I don't have a problem." Grace said, "So why did you just bump into them like that!" Robbie looked away and responded that he did not know, and she slapped his face turning it to her. She said, "As long as you live you better not ever turn away from me you look at me while I am talking to you do you understand me!" Already hurt and in shock, he responded, "Yes ma'am." She stared at him and told him to apologize to his siblings for bumping them. Robbie apologized, and Grace told him to get his hateful ass out of her house and go to school. Anthony grinned. When the children headed out, Grace asked Anthony, "What's wrong with that boy? He sure is changing." He replied, "Baby I have no idea but the next time he does something like that I will handle it if it's ok with you because he is acting too damn mannish around here and there is only one man in this house!" She replied back to him, "Baby, you know that it's ok with me, you are his step daddy and you help me raise these kids so if you have to discipline him then you have my permission to do that."

That day, Robbie started with a bad attitude towards his siblings. While they walked to school, they all stared at him and he angrily confronted them saying, "What are ya'll looking at! Stop looking at me, ya'll make me sick and I hate ya'll so go home at tell mommy and that bitch Anthony that because I don't care he is not my daddy anyway!" In shock, they all looked at him and started crying, Tori headed back towards the house and screamed saying that she was going to tell their mom until Robbie chased her down, begging her not to do it. He said "Sister please don't tell it, I am sorry I was mad, I don't hate ya'll, what do you want of mine I will give you anything?" she looked at him said "Ok brother I don't want nothing I just don't like when you said that you hate us because mommy said that brothers and sisters are supposed to get along no matter what." Robbie asked for their forgiveness and they all agreed as long as he agreed to be nice to them from then on.

Robbie had been through so much at that point that he noticed that the stress was changing him he was mean and he'd also become very guarded.

CHAPTER
10

One day at school, after being beaten by Anthony, Robbie was sitting at his desk, taking a spelling test. He was very good at spelling, he'd won the local spelling bee, two years in a row. But on this particular day, he was going through the test and the word, "King" was listed. This made him think about how Anthony often called himself the King and just the thought of that word caused an emotional reaction in Robbie. He sat at his desk and suddenly started stabbing his spelling test, while yelling and screaming. The teacher went running over to him, frightened by this unexpected fit of rage. She hugged Robbie tight until he calmed down, asking what was wrong. Robbie's only response was that he hated the word "King." He was then escorted to the principal's office for disrupting the class. During the walk there, Robbie began to mentally prepare himself for what would come next. He fully expected to be beaten once Grace and Anthony found out about his outburst. He started whispering to himself, saying "Don't be afraid, he can't hurt you anymore" over and over again.

Mr. Jones, the principal, walked up to Robbie and stared at him for a moment, his brow furrowed and a look of concern on his face. Then he asked Robbie to come inside his office to talk about what had happened. Robbie sat in silence for a while, not sure how to respond because he knew that if he spoke too much, his true feelings would be revealed and all that he was going through might just rush out of his mouth. Mr. Jones eventually started to get annoyed with Robbie because he refused to give an explanation. So, he advised that he would be contacting his mother which could make matters even worse for him. Robbie continued to sit quietly, not responding to anything that Mr. Jones said. Shortly after Mr. Jones called Grace, she arrived, visibly upset. When she walked into the office everybody got quiet and the receptionist greeted her asking if how she could help. Grace's only response was "Where is he?" Whenever Grace would get really upset, her tone of voice would be really low, and the next level would be pure rage. Robbie's heart began to pound in anticipation of Grace's response to seeing him. He knew that she had been contacted during her work day, resulting in her having to leave her job to come to the school. She had always told her children that if she ever had to leave work for anything concerning school that was bad, they would regret it. Mr. Jones heard Grace, went to the front of the office and invited her into his office, informing that Robbie was back there with him. As she approached, he asked how she was doing, and she gave no response, she just looked at Robbie, walked in and sat beside him, giving him the stare from hell!

Robbie's heart was beating so fast that he thought he was having a panic attack. Mr. Page said, "Miss Philips, this is what happened, Robbie..." Grace stopped him in the middle of his explanation, looked at Robbie and screamed, "NO!! I want you to tell me what happened!"

He was so startled that he nearly pissed his pants. He looked down at the floor, because he couldn't look her in the eye. Grace grabbed his chin, yanked it towards her and said, "Boy, look at me when I am talking to you and you better tell me right now what happened before I put my foot in your little red ass!" Tears immediately started to roll down his cheeks, he knew he needed to try to explain why he did what he did. Robbie looked at Grace, and said with a stutter, "I was taking the spelling test and I knew that I was going to do good on his test, then I saw the word king and I stopped because I didn't like that word, it made me very mad and I started stabbing my test." She pulled away from him, sitting back in the chair, stood up over him and responded, "So you want to throw a fit and you don't know why huh?" Robbie tried to explain that he hadn't thrown a fit, telling her she'd never understand. But Grace was no longer interested in any explanations. She snatched Robbie up and started to whip him right there in front of Mr. Jones.

Grace was a solid, heavy handed country woman who was as strong as an ox so when she hit someone, they felt it all. Mr. Jones was so afraid to stop her from beating Robbie that he put his head down and allowed her to finish what she started. Suddenly, Robbie began to laugh while he was being beaten which made Grace even angrier. Both she and Mr. Jones were so stunned by Robbie's reaction to the beating that they paused and just stared at him in disbelief and Grace told him to sit down. Robbie just looked at his mother, telling her that she would never understand. Explaining that he wasn't able to feel pain any longer, apologizing to her and assuring that he would never misbehave in school again. Grace took his hand, placing it on hers and said, "Son what is going on with you, tell me what I am missing, what are you hiding from me? I need to know son." Robbie didn't explain anything further, so she decided to let things be so that she could get back to work. Mr. Jones was stunned by what had taken place, and he could sense that something was going on with Robbie emotionally. Before she left, Mr. Jones had assured Grace that he would keep an eye on Robbie to make sure that he was back to normal.

Robbie knew that his outburst had made things slightly more complicated for him as his mother and Mr. Jones would both be keeping a close eye on his behaviors to figure out what was going on. He also knew that he would be in for another beating once Anthony found out that he had gotten into trouble at school that day. When the school day came to an end, he packed his bag and began to walk out of the building. Mr. Jones was waiting at the door to speak with Robbie and ask him more questions. Robbie tried his best to avoid Mr. Jones but he caught him, calling him back to speak with him. Robbie knew he was trying to figure out what was happening with him, so he responded saying "Ok, but I really don't want to talk about it".

As he waited to speak with Mr. Jones, he noticed his classmates staring and whispering about him. Then he watched parents came to pick their kids up, observing how happy they were to see them. Kids ran up to their fathers hugging them and being embraced back. Robbie started to get sad because he had always dreamed of having a father to be there to pick him up from school, show love, and make him feel happy. He never did have a good relationship with his biological father, he was around but was very inconsistent to the point where, in his mind, he'd lost him. He knew that it was very unlikely that his father would ever be able to give him what he prayed for. And although he looked just like his father, and he had no relationship with him, he wanted to be just like him in other ways. Robbie idolized his father in ways similar to how he'd idolized his mother. Robbie's father was amazing to him, as strong and muscular as a superhero, he was good at entertaining everyone, he was good at everything he did, and he was very athletic and popular. Robbie occasionally found himself looking in the mirror, trying to imitate him even though his father barely talked to him whenever he saw him.

Finally, Mr. Jones came to the bench, sat beside him, placing his hand on Robbie's shoulder saying, "What do you like to do in your spare time?" Robbie was hesitant to answer him, he didn't trust him or anybody for that matter. He felt as though Mr. Jones was trying to pry into his personal life so that he could find out what was really going on. Grace had always told him to never tell the people anything about what goes on in her house, so he'd already made up his mind that he would not tell him the truth about anything. He let his childlike imagination take over and decided to make up a story to tell him. He told Mr. Jones that he liked riding his bike, playing with his sisters and brother, watching TV with his mother, cooking and going to the park with his family. That didn't seem to do enough to quell Mr. Jones' concerns, he asked if anyone was inside the household besides Robbie's mother and siblings. Robbie replied explaining that his mother had a husband, "Mr. Anthony." Which prompted him to ask Robbie about him, he asked what Mr. Anthony does, as if he was trying to gather his thoughts about him. Robbie only responded saying "I don't know, he is just there, I don't really talk to him like that." It seemed like Mr. Jones was beginning to have suspicions related to Anthony but decided to back off the subject when he saw a look of fear on Robbie's face when being questioned about him. He said, "I'll tell you what, how about me and you go to get ice cream tomorrow after school if it's ok with your mother." That put a big smile on Robbie's face, he responded excitedly saying "Yes sir! I would love that!" He jumped up, gave Mr. Jones a high five and headed home.

Robbie was so happy about the idea of having ice cream with his principal that he skipped and sang all the way home. It was like Christmas because he was rarely able to do fun things. He had grown accustomed to being stuck in the house most of the time and being mistreated by Anthony. It would be like an escape to have someone take the time to show him one on one attention and take him to have a treat. As Robbie got closer to home, his happy thoughts turned sour in anticipation of what was to come. It had gotten so that he had to become a different person when he was at home, for his own sanity. All he could see was darkness, like a shadow that hovered above the house. Trying to cope with the abuse he experienced, Robbie began to disassociate, taking on three personalities. He became Batman when Anthony was beating him, Superman when he was able to protect his siblings from the abuse, and He-Man whenever he was locked in the closet and starved. This was the only thing that seemed to help prevent Robbie from completely crumbling emotionally.

Robbie struggled with self-worth, being made to feel like I was the worst kid in the world, by Anthony. He developed very low self-esteem, which also impacted how he saw himself when he looked in the mirror. Robbie was continually in a depressive and anxious state, and suicidal in the moments that he wanted to give up. He'd frequently thought about running in front of a cars, with the hopes of being killed instantly. He also thought about overdosing on something or poisoning himself by drinking bleach then hiding so that nobody would be able to find him in time to help. Robbie didn't know how to swim so he had also thought about jumping in the local lake to drown himself. As he reached the front yard he began to feel butterflies in his stomach thinking about whether Grace had told Anthony what he had done at school that day.

Robbie looked up when he heard voices coming from the front porch and looked up to see Anthony and his friends. Anthony was a con artist, so he put on a show in front of everybody to make himself look good, which Robbie hated with a passion. Anthony's friends all shook Robbie's hand, greeting him, to which Robbie responded but his goal was to get past them quickly and have as little interaction with him as possible. Anthony stepped right in front of him though, blocking his path, reaching out to hug him, saying "What's up son? How was school?" Robbie was disgusted but decided to play along out of fear, so he responded "Hey, it was ok I did the well on my spelling test." He is rubbed his head and responded, "Yeah son I heard about that, you know we need to talk right?" Robbie turned back and nodded in agreement but as he walked away, he heard Anthony's friend saying how great of a step dad he was and how they wanted to be just like him.

Robbie knew it was time to prepare himself for the torture session that he was about to go through because he now had no doubts about whether or not his mother had told Anthony about what happened. He also figured that Anthony knew the significance of him stabbing the word king on his paper. He looked around nervously for his sibling, but they weren't home, and the nervousness turned to panic because he knew it was just the two of them in the house. Robbie sat on the edge of the bed trying to think of why they were not there, and it finally came to him that they'd stayed after school for an event. He felt his body shaking with fear, afraid that his life would be over because this man was about to beat him to death. Then he allowed the numbness to take over because there was nothing he could do to avoid the beating, so he decided he needed to take the beating like a warrior. Then he thought of writing a letter to his mother, in case he didn't survive. In the letter he was very descriptive of everything that had happened to him up and until that point. He didn't know where to hide the letter, but he knew it would have to be somewhere that Grace and his siblings would find it. Tears rolled down his eyes as he wrote the terrible things he'd experienced, and it made him realize just how bad it all had been. He had to stop writing and decided that he had to survive, he couldn't allow things to end like this. All of a sudden, he felt a really strong feeling, got up and walked to the door where Anthony was with his friends and stood there looking at him. In that moment he decided to use Anthony's "good stepfather act" to his advantage.

Robbie headed to the door and Anthony's friend tapped him on the shoulder and to let him know that Robbie was standing there. Anthony looked up and asked, "What is it son? What's wrong?" Robbie replied, "Nothing, I finished my homework and I was wondering if I could go and play with my friends down the street." He looked at him as if he knew what Robbie was up to but had to play the role of a good dad and he said, "Son, if your homework is done then you know that I don't have a problem with you going to play, just be careful and make sure that you are back in the house before it gets dark." Robbie responded, thanking him, and ran out quickly though he did not know where to go because he had no friends, but Anthony didn't know that.

Robbie took off down the street and did not look back, the only thing that he could hope for was that Grace would be home by the time that he got back so that he could avoid the torture. This was like vacation for him, he was free with no worries, but he had to find somewhere to go because he really didn't want to end up running into one of Anthony's friends who might tell him that they'd saw him just roaming the streets alone. Robbie saw a path in the woods and began to follow the path to wherever it would lead him. This was an adventure for him because it was rare that he had opportunities to be alone and enjoy himself at same time. Life had always been full of seriousness and responsibility for him. So, he decided to take advantage of the free time he'd been given. His imagination and excitement took over as he walked down the path, things began to turn into a mission. He had always wanted to be a super-hero and save the world so as he embarked on his adventure he decided he would see things as if they were obstacles for him to overcome so that he could complete the mission.

The trees were swaying, the birds were chirping, insects were creeping along the ground, and Robbie was just happy to be out in nature. Then he looked up and saw a rabbit being chased by a big gray cat. They were running so fast and quick that his eyes couldn't keep up. He felt as if the cat was like Anthony and the rabbit was like him. If the rabbit needed his help, he was willing to do anything to help stop the cat from killing it. He followed as they ran, running faster and faster to catch up. Periodically, the rabbit would stop and take a break and the cat would try it's best to quietly creep up on him but could never catch up to the rabbit. The cat seemed to get frustrated with not being able to capture its prey, so it gave up and went in another direction.

Seeing this interaction made Robbie think about himself and Anthony again. Robbie was definitely the rabbit, faster, smarter, and better prepared than Anthony, the cat. He was always trying to outsmart Robbie, to find a reason to punish him. But Robbie knew he had to be faster on his feet than Anthony. He had to think fast and be ready for him. The forest was peaceful. He'd moved to stand closer to the lake, while listening to the water flowing, birds chirping, and the wind blow, softly. For the first time in a long time, Robbie felt a feeling of peace. There was nothing bothering him, no siblings to argue with, and no Anthony. He saw a big tree standing alone close by the lake, it had beautiful leaves and it looked so peaceful that he had to go sit down, up against the tree to watch the water. Being there, surrounded by nature, was so calming to his soul, he had never experienced peace like this before. He laid his head against the tree, closed his eyes and started to think. His thoughts were all over the place, from wanting to run away, to wanting to jump in the lake and kill himself just so that he wouldn't have to deal with Anthony again. If he had jumped no one would find him, if he went back, Anthony would probably beat him to death, and if he ran away he would starve. Robbie didn't really want to die because he also thought about how it would hurt his mother and siblings, so he had to get those thoughts out of his mind. Robbie loved them so much. He knew that if something happened to him, Anthony would start to take it out on his siblings and he could not let that happen. Robbie began to cry, feeling as if there was no choice that would result in his being safe and happy. As he sat there, he felt time slipping away, as it got later into the evening he knew he needed to leave soon and head home. Before he left, Robbie decided to designate this as his new hideout, that he would call "Happy Ville". It was getting darker outside, so he sped up his pace, trying to get home and he soon arrived to see Grace's car in the front of the yard.

CHAPTER
11

Robbie walked inside the house and noticed his mother and siblings sitting in the living room watching television. Grace said, "Hey son, did you have fun with your friends?" To which Robbie replied, "Yes mommy I had so much fun!" He was looking around for Anthony to appear, but he didn't, he wasn't home. Grace looked beautiful, happy, and peaceful as she sat there with all of them and this was how Robbie wished things would stay. He didn't think that his mom needed a man at all, and definitely not Anthony! She seemed like a different, better person when he was not around. As the children watched television Grace said to them, "After this show goes off we need to clean up a little bit before you all go to bed."

Everyone agreed except for Robbie who was confused because the kitchen and living room were all clean before they had left for school that day, so it must have been Anthony who messed things up. Robbie told his mom his thoughts about Anthony messing up the house and Grace sat on the edge of the couch screaming, "Boy you are not grown! When I say shit need to be done in this house then that's what the hell I mean! I don't give a damn who messed it up do you understand me?" Robbie was angry but didn't want to stay on Grace's bad side, plus he had gotten in trouble at school that day. So, he responded "Yes ma'am, I will clean up everything." She sat back in the chair and went back to the normal, happy peaceful mother mode that she was in before he made her go from zero to one hundred really quick! The show went off and Grace said, "Ok mama's babies let's get to work, I am about to turn on some music."

Now this the children loved to do because they all loved music, and dancing which was a trait that they'd inherited from their mother. Robbie went and got the broom because I loved to sweep, his siblings picked the duties that they loved to do, and his mom went to the record player and put on her favorite Album "The Heat Is On" released in 1975 by the "Isley Brothers". The children knew this whole album because Grace played it very often. Her favorite song was "For the Love of You" and she would sing and dance around the house without a care in the world, full of joy and happiness. The reason Robbie loved to sweep was because he always wanted to be Michael Jackson, so he would pretend that the broom was his microphone and that he was performing for the world. He would sweep, stop, then dance and sing. Grace would always come and dance with Robbie as he swept the floor. This was the best feeling in the world because he knew that Grace was in her element even for this little bit of time she was happy, content, glowing, and was able to enjoy herself. Seeing Grace this way brought so much joy to his heart. When their mother was happy, the children were happy, when she was sad the children were sad. Robbie put the broom down and took Grace's hand to dance like they were on top of the world, with all the children singing "Living for the love of you!"

Grace had an amazing personality, and she was so funny, as she imitated the song! The children all were cleaning, laughing and having a good time when Robbie thought he heard someone at the door. His mom asked what was wrong, he said, "I thought I heard someone at the door but never mind." So, they continued to dance and enjoy themselves and as Robbie danced with Grace, and did a spin, he turned around and noticed Anthony standing in the door way. He had the meanest, ugliest look on his face. Robbie stopped in his tracks and put his head down, Grace looked up, and said, "Hey Baby I didn't know you were here we were just cleaning up come on." She tried to take his hand to dance with him, but he pulled away from her saying that he had a bad headache. Robbie knew the real reason, but as soon as he mentioned his headache, Grace's whole mood changed. She went from being happy and jolly into taking care of Anthony's spoiled ass! Robbie sat, sulking, thinking she cut their time short because Anthony was upset about seeing him dance with his mother. If Robbie could've slapped him, in that moment, he would have knocked his face off.

Grace told everyone to finish cleaning, and she turned the record player off, telling them to keep the noise down and hurry up and finish so that they could take a bath and go to bed. She took Anthony to the room, rubbed his back and said, "I am about to take care of his poor, big ole baby." This made Robbie so sick to his stomach, Anthony had Grace wrapped around his finger! There was nothing that he couldn't get away with and he knew it. Robbie was beginning to feel like his mother had turned against her children to please this man. He had tried so hard not to be mad at Grace, but it was getting to the point to where he was developing animosity towards her. He hoped that Grace would eventually see Anthony's true colors.

CHAPTER
12

One day after school, Robbie and Jake were walking home, and Jake was talking about wanting to be a zoo keeper when he grew up, Robbie asked him why he would want to do that because zoo keepers don't make good money. Jake replied, "Yes they do, Anthony told me that I would be rich if I want to become one!" Robbie rolled his eyes, annoyed that Jake would listen to anything that Anthony said and responded, "Fuck him! He broke anyway he can't tell you nothing about being rich!" Jake stood wide eyed, his mouth open in a big 'o' shape. He said, "I am going to tell that you cussed and that you were talking about Anthony!" Robbie, enraged grabbed Jake by his arm, made him walk to the woods so that nobody and see and told him to get on his knees. Jake was afraid and asked Robbie why he was doing this, Robbie shouted at him "Just do it! You want to go and tell on me then I am going to teach you a lesson that you will never forget!" Jake was terrified and it made Robbie feel good that he scared him although he had never felt that way before. Robbie wanted to feel like he was in charge, he wanted to feel like a king, and he wanted Jake to feel what he felt when Anthony abused him. Jake listened to his brother and got on his knees, Robbie then placed his hand on the back of Jake's neck asking him "Are you going to tell on me?" Jake didn't respond so Robbie hit him on the back of the head and he started to scream. Then he put his hand over Jake's mouth and told him that if he made another sound he would really make him hurt. Then he asked Jake again if he was going to tell on him and Jake looked up with tears running down his face responding that no, he wouldn't. Robbie then squeezed his neck harder and said, "NO WHAT?" Jake said, "No Sir" and Robbie smiled because he felt mean and powerful.

Afterwards it occurred to Robbie that he was really starting to lose his mind and become someone that he didn't like. Jake had jumped up and took off running as fast as he could to get home. Robbie had wanted to know how it felt to be the King, to put fear into someone else's heart and for his brother Jake to see how it felt to be him. And even as he pondered the realization that his personality was changing, he had devious thoughts of doing more to hurt to Jake and it felt good to think about hurting someone. Robbie began to feel afraid. A thought flashed of his grandmother who always told him "to never let the devil think he has won", that Robbie was "covered under the blood of Jesus" and to pray whenever he felt the devil winning. Robbie thought to himself, "I feel powerful, I feel amazing, and like I'm on top of the world from hurting someone I love. That's definitely the devil winning!" It hit him hard. He thought about everything that Anthony had done to him, how he felt, how it hurt and changed him, then he thought about how his brother must've felt when he did those things to him and suddenly he began to cry tears of remorse.

There was a park nearby called Freeborn St with a merry go round that Robbie loved to ride. He ran to the park and went straight towards it, turning it as fast as he could, he jumped on, dropped to his knees and prayed for GOD to not let him turn in to a devil like Anthony. As he prayed, he felt a sense of calm come over him. Laying on his back as the merry go round took spun around it felt like it would never stop so he closed his eyes and let his thoughts drift away. Robbie imagined playing in a big yard with his siblings, the children were dressed in all white, and happy, Grace was standing on the porch of an enormous house watching them play and there was a tall dark-skinned man standing behind her, he was huge, big hands, very muscular, shaved very clean and dressed to perfection. He looked nothing like Anthony who dressed like a thug.

In his day dream the man seemed to have made Grace and the children happier than they'd ever been. Suddenly the feeling of rain drops on his face snapped Robbie back to reality. It had started to thunderstorm and he'd fallen asleep on the merry go round at the park. He didn't know how long he had been there but he knew that he had to get home fast because his little brother had no key to get into the house. Jake was probably there all alone which was the last thing that Robbie wanted, especially after what he had done to him earlier. Robbie sprinted home as fast as he could, soaking wet from the rain and hearing thunder on the horizon. The lightning and thunder was so loud that it sounded like bombs exploding. His heart pounded in his chest as he ran to get home. All he could think

43

about was Jake being alone and afraid and he wasn't there. Finally, Robbie could see the house in the distance, but as he got closer he didn't see Jake and he began to panic. He thought to himself, "Why did I leave and let him walk home alone, what am I going to do?"

Robbie quickly ran through the front yard, yelling for Jake, and went around to check the back yard. He was nowhere to be found. He ran to the side of the house and still didn't see Jake anywhere, so I slowly walked to the front of the house and as he looked up, he noticed Jake standing in the doorway with Anthony standing behind him. This was the worst possible outcome. Nothing could have prepared him for Anthony being home this early. Robbie stood in the rain, afraid to go inside, he Jake, and put his head down. He didn't want to look at Anthony because it would make things worse. Anthony told Jake to go to his room and finish his homework, then looked at Robbie and said, "You just let your brother walk home by himself huh?" Robbie responded shaking his head no. Anthony said, "You a mothafucking lie little nigga! What I tell you about lying to me? Get your ass up here on this porch and look at me now!" The tears began to fall from his eyes as Robbie slowly started towards the porch, making Anthony angrier. He said, "So you want to take your time and disrespect me?" he stormed out the door, grabbing Robbie by the arm. In one swift motion he picked Robbie up by his neck and slammed him on the floor of the porch like a WWF wrestler. Then he put his bare foot on Robbie's mouth telling him "You got my feet wet and dirty, clean that shit off!" Robbie started trying to wipe the mud off of Anthony's foot and he slapped him hard telling him to put his hands down. Anthony put his foot back on Robbie's mouth saying, "I said you got my fucking feet wet and dirty, now clean that shit off with your mouth!"

Robbie was furious and disgusted with the idea of licking mud off of Anthony's toes, so he just stared up at him angrily. He knew his refusal would make Anthony even more violent towards him, but he didn't care. Today was the day that he was going to let him know that he was tired of being afraid of him and that he would have to kill him if that's what he wanted to do. Anthony kicked Robbie in his side, hard, 3 times and Robbie still didn't move. He said "So you want to be a man huh? You think I won't kill your little ass out here huh? I don't give a fuck about going to jail little nigga I will kill you and everybody!" Then he moved his foot to

Robbie's throat and pressed down on it until he couldn't breathe. Just when Robbie thought he was going to die and was nearly blacking out from lack of oxygen, Jake ran out and screamed for him to stop. Anthony pulled his foot up, as Robbie gasped for air holding his throat. Anthony yelled at Jake, "Take your little ass in the house!" then turned as if he was going after him. Robbie couldn't let Anthony hurt Jake, he knew that if he did what Anthony wanted him to do, he would feel powerful and leave Jake alone. Robbie grabbed Anthony by his leg, he kicked him off, but Robbie pleaded with him, saying, "Please let me clean your feet, please just leave him alone I will clean your feet."

He stopped, looked at Robbie and said, "Lil nigga you got a lot of heart!" He punched him in the chest then pushed him back down on the floor, placed his foot back on Robbie's mouth and said, "Clean them real good boy!" Robbie licked the mud and dirt off his foot and as he did, Anthony taunted him, saying "I told you I am the King, yeah lick them good, get all the dirt off too it better be spic and span and hurry the fuck up before I make you do this all over again!" Robbie felt so violated, he was in so much pain, not just physically but mentally. Sucking on a man's toes after being punched, choked, slammed, and there was nothing that he could do about it because this man was crazy enough to kill him. After Robbie finished licking his toes, he looked at his feet and said, "Good Job Son, now get your ass up take a bath and do your homework" Robbie said, "Yes Sir" and headed inside.

Once they were in the house, Anthony called Jake, telling him to come into his room. Robbie stood in front of the door, refusing to move. He was not about to let Anthony harm his brother. Anthony looked at him and said, "Boy do what the fuck I told you to do before you come see me again, I am not going to touch your punk ass brother now go on!" Robbie slowly walked away, and Jake stared at him with tears in his eyes as he passed him in the hall. He stood and waited at the end of the hall just close enough so that he could hear him talking to Jake. He still wasn't convinced that Anthony wouldn't try to hurt him, so he was prepared to run in there if need be. Jake walked into the room and Anthony said, "Son everything is going to be ok, me and your brother was just playing, we weren't serious, so you have nothing to worry about ok." Jake said, "Yes sir" Anthony said, "You know I love all ya'll and I would never hurt ya'll right?" To which

Jake responded, "Yes Sir, I love you too." Robbie felt sick to his stomach to hear him say that, he could not believe that Jake let this man lie to him when he knew that it wasn't true! He knew that they weren't playing, but he said that he loved this man.

Robbie felt so stupid for protecting his brother, just for him to turn on him the way he did. He stood in the bathroom, staring into the mirror, wondering why he was being targeted, and why Anthony hated him so much. He didn't want to live anymore because he felt like it was only going to get worse and eventually he would end up killing him. Robbie wanted a way out, but he knew that his mom wouldn't believe him. He believed that there was nothing he could do to physically to beat him up, but he knew that he was mentally stronger than him. Robbie was a fighter and knew that he had to keep fighting until something happened to Anthony. He touched his face and then touched the mirror so that he could focus and said to himself, "You are not weak, you will never be a bitch or a punk and fuck Anthony he is nothing to you! Take his life!" Robbie smiled to himself with tears in his eyes and started to take his bath so that he could get to his homework.

When Robbie came out of the bathroom he could hear Anthony on the phone whispering with someone and it wasn't a male. He was telling this person that he really wanted to see them and that he was sorry for hitting her it was an accident, then he asked her could he come over to make it up to her. Robbie wasn't surprised by hearing this because he knew the type of person Anthony was. He had already cheated on Grace and he knew that Anthony was abusive even though he had not abused Grace, or so he thought. Robbie took what he heard and added it to his plan of how he was going to end Anthony. He knew that Grace would be home soon, so he had to hurry to finish his homework and get his chores done. Robbie felt like the man of the house because Anthony was so spoiled by Grace. He never cooked, cleaned, fixed anything, but Grace was so in love with him. Robbie was more of a man than he was, when things were broken, he figured out how to fix them. Robbie would also start dinner before his mom got home and she would finish. He cleaned the house, took out the trash, cut the grass, got his siblings ready for school, helped them with their homework, and put them to bed. As he finished his homework started to do his chores, Jake came into the kitchen, took his hand and whispered,

"I am sorry brother, I don't believe him, and I really hate him". Robbie responded, telling him that it was ok, he wasn't mad anymore and they would just need to pray for things to get better.

Jake was very quiet, but he was smart and knew what was going on. He knew that Anthony was abusing Robbie, but he was afraid, and he also wanted a father figure in the house. Laura and Tori had finally gotten home from school, they came inside, spoke to Anthony then went to their room. After a few minutes, Laura, the oldest sister came to the edge of her door and signaled for Robbie to come to their room, he put the broom down and walked over to her. She put her index finger up against her mouth, signaling him to be quiet and told him to whisper, then asked if he was ok. Robbie responded, nodding his head yes, not understanding why she was asking him this. Laura put her hand on his shoulder and said, "Miss Suzie told me to tell you to come to see her but go to her back yard so that nobody will see you." Robbie asked her why and she responded, "I don't know why, but she told me that she saw you get hurt." Robbie said, "Ok sis thanks I will."

CHAPTER
13

Miss Suzie was their neighbor across the street, she was about 65 year's old, a nice elderly lady who was extremely nosey. She knew everything that went on because she watched everyone's houses from her window. Robbie was nervous and didn't know how he would manage to sneak out of the house to see Miss Suzie. He put on his tennis shoes and started towards the back door, before he left he had to peep into the room Anthony was in to make sure that he was occupied. He tip toed to peak around the corner of his room and there he was sound asleep and snoring like a hibernating bear. But Robbie knew he had to be fast. He made it across the first yard and their dog was in the house, so he was good to make it quietly past all of the other yards and crossed the street to head to Miss Suzie's back yard.

Robbie was hesitant because he didn't know what to expect but he was already there and couldn't turn back now. He went up to the door and knocked quietly, he could hear her singing Tina Turner's song "What's Love Got To Do With It" so he didn't think that she'd heard him at the door. Robbie knocked again but she continued to sing. He was getting tired of waiting out there and figured it wasn't meant for him to come over there so turned and started to walk off.

It bothered him that he'd gone through all of the trouble to get there but he wasn't willing to stand there any longer waiting. As Robbie got to the edge of her back yard he heard a voice say, "Hey Sweetie, where are you going?" He turned around and it was Miss Suzie. He said, "I was going home, I had knocked on your door and you didn't answer." She said, "Sweetie you have to knock hard, I done got old I can't hear like I used to." Robbie apologized and said, "My sister told me that you wanted to see me." Miss Suzie looked him up and down as if she was sad and concerned making him feel uncomfortable and said, "Yes I sent for you sweetie, there is something very important that we need to talk about but first let me ask you this, are you ok?" Robbie took a step back, looked away and said, "Yes

Ma'am, I am ok." Miss Suzie put her hand on his face, looked him dead in his eyes and said, "No you are not sweetie and it's not ok."

He was trying to wrap his head around what she was talking about, because she never really talked interacted with him before today. Robbie looked down towards his feet and said, "I don't know what you are talking about Miss Suzie, I am ok." She put her hands on her hips, sighed and said, "How long has this been going on? I know that man that your mother is with has been beating you, I saw what happened in the yard earlier today and I know that if he did that outside in the open, that it wasn't his first time." Robbie was shocked, he didn't know what to say, this was the first time that somebody had witnessed the abuse. He couldn't lie and deny what happened, she had seen it herself. So, he looked at her and responded, "A long time." Miss Suzie took his hands and squeezed them and saying, "My God, my God protect this child from that man." Robbie explained to her that he'd never told anyone because Anthony threatened to hurt his family. She was floored, she said, "That's exactly why I didn't call the police when I saw that man beating you like that because I have been there before, and I didn't want you to go through what I went through. I wanted to talk to you first and let you know that you can't keep letting this man do this to you." Robbie was in tears, there had never been anyone to talk to about this, it was something that he inside, so it felt good to let his feelings out. Miss Suzie looked at him and said, "That man beat you like an animal and threw you like a rag doll, it hurt my heart to see that he would do that to a young child! You have to tell your mom sweetie, because it's only going to get worse." Robbie responded, "My mom won't believe me, she is crazy about him he has her wrapped around his finger, I don't know who else I could tell." Miss Suzie asked if Anthony also abused his siblings. Robbie shook his head no and said "I don't know why, it's like he hated me from the very first time that he saw me. I never did anything to him." Miss Suzie just explained that some people were just sick in the head and it has nothing to do with hating anybody. Robbie said, "He says that he is the King and I am his servant, all he does is beat me up. Before he came I did everything then and with him in the house I still do everything, I just don't understand."

Miss Suzie was getting upset about the awful things that Robbie was telling her, she explained to him that Anthony felt threatened by him and he was nothing but a punk. She told Robbie that if he ever needed to talk, he could stop by and see her. Robbie cried and cried, it was a relief to be able to tell someone. He told Miss Suzie that he had to get home. She really didn't want him to go, and that she really appreciated him coming over. Before he walked out, she gave him a big hug that reminded him of his grandmother's hugs. Robbie smiled and said, "Miss Suzie, thank you so much for everything, I will make sure that I stop over if I need to talk. I am scared but I know that I have to be strong!" She looked at him, smiled and said, "See sweetie, God is already working it out all you have to do is pray and have faith and watch God work! Now you go head and get home before that demon wakes up, ok." Robbie said, "Yes Ma'am!" and headed towards the back door to go back the same way that he came. The rain had stopped which was good because he didn't want to track mud into the house.

Everything that Miss Suzie said to him kept replaying in his mind, over and over again. Robbie knew that God had his back, so he wasn't alone anymore, Miss Suzie had given him hope. As he got closer to the house, he smelled cigarette smoke. Anthony was in the front yard which meant that he probably didn't even know that Robbie was gone. He quickly snuck through the back door and went to his room. His siblings were in the living room watching television, which meant that they were done with their chores and homework.

As Robbie sat on his bed, Laura came in and said, "Anthony didn't know you were gone so don't worry because we didn't tell on you brother." Robbie said, "Ok thanks sister!" Laura was very nosey, so he already knew what she was about to ask next. She stared at him as if he had something to tell her, so he turned his head to the side, looked at her and said, "What is it? Why are you looking at me like that?" She smiled and said, "Tell me what Miss Angie said please." Robbie was annoyed by her questioning and he didn't completely trust her with anything that he had to tell. He laid back on the bed, put his hands over his forehead and said, "She said that she wants me to help her with her yard." Laura looked as if she knew he wasn't telling the truth and said, "So she called you all the way over there to ask you to help her with her yard? Do I look like I have a big S on my forehead? What did she really want to talk about? If you don't tell me I will tell mom." This was exactly what Robbie expected Laura to say because that was the type of person she was. He knew he had to tell her something exciting enough for her to leave him alone, but he was not going to tell her the truth. He didn't trust her to keep a secret. Finally, after thinking for a few minutes, he told her that Miss Suzie asked him to start going to the store for her when she needed him and that she would pay two dollars every time that he went. Laura seemed to believe him this time because she finally left him alone.

After his chores, Robbie sat and thought about a plan for getting rid of Anthony. He knew that if he told anyone about what he had been doing, he would need proof and the only witness was Miss Suzie. One idea Robbie had was to start provoking Anthony to abuse him in front of people, so that he would have more witnesses besides Miss Suzie. Another thought was trying to record him talking to his mistress and giving the recording to Grace, but he wasn't sure that would work either. While he was lost in his thoughts and plans, Robbie heard his mother's car pull up in the yard. Robbie heard Grace call his name but didn't come out of his room right away because he knew it irritated Anthony for him to hear Grace call for him.

Robbie waited until the second time Graced called him to reply, "Yes Mom!" She replied back, "Boy you better come out and give your mama a hug!" This was heaven to him, just to hear her say that, he ran out with the biggest smile on his face. Grace was standing in front of her room where Anthony was which was perfect because Robbie wanted him to see Grace give him a hug. Grace looked as beautiful as ever and Robbie ran up and gave her the biggest hug, then looked around to see Anthony giving him an evil glare. Robbie loved every bit of it. Grace grabbed his face and felt him slightly pull away because he didn't want her to see that his lip was busted and that he was hurt from what Anthony had done. She put her hand on his shoulder, turned her head to the side and she looked at him as if she knew something was wrong, then she said, "Baby what happened to your lip, it look swollen?" Robbie looked at Anthony then looked at her and said, "I fell mom." Jake ran up and said, "Anthony was playing with Robbie mama that's how it happened." Robbie's heart dropped, he had no idea that Jake would say that.

Grace looked back at Anthony, frowned, looked back at Robbie, touched his mouth and said, "Open your mouth up boy!" Robbie reluctantly opened his mouth because he knew that it wasn't going to be good and when she saw that he had a big gash on the inside of his mouth. Anthony stood up and said, "Baby let me explain." It was too late Grace was furious, she looked at Anthony and said, "What the hell happened to my child because this shit right here is not a playing matter!" Anthony tried to speak but was quickly interrupted by Grace, she pointed at him while looking at Robbie, saying, "Wait a minute, why did you lie to when if all you and Anthony was doing was so called playing?" Robbie didn't know what to say, this was his chance to spill it all, but he was speechless, so he just responded that he didn't know. Grace turned around to him, put her bag down, put her hand on her hip and she said, "Now let me tell you something, I don't know what the hell happened to my child, but I don't play when it comes to anybody harming my kids! I don't give a damn who you are, so you best get to explaining because somebody is going to die up in here tonight whether it's me or you!"

Robbie was shocked, this was something new to see Grace go into a rage over something happening to him, he was so happy! He knew Anthony had some tricks up his sleeve, so he was prepared to hear what he had to say to Grace about the situation this time. Anthony walked up to Grace slowly and he started laughing. Grace looked at him and said, "What the fuck is funny Anthony, I don't see why in the hell you are laughing I will fuck you up in here tonight! He stopped laughing, smiled and said, "Baby calm your mean ass down, he told me that he wanted me to teach him how to wrestle like the wrestlers on TV and I was showing him some of the moves when I accidentally hit him in his mouth, I didn't know it was that bad." He then looked at Robbie saying, "I apologize son, I didn't know that I did that, why didn't you tell me you were hurt." Robbie was wondering if he should spill it all now or if it would back fire on him. He'd thought about this a million times, Anthony had Grace wrapped too tight, so he had to go with the fake story for now. Robbie looked at Anthony and said, "I didn't know it was that bad until right before mom came home." Jake stormed off angrily rolling his eyes because he knew Robbie was lying.

Grace still didn't one hundred percent believe this story simply because Robbie had lied about it initially, but for now she took their word for it. She inspected Robbie's busted lip again, then looked him in the eyes and said, "You know I'm your mama, right?" Robbie responded, "Yes ma'am." She said, "You know that I know my kids and I know that you are not telling me the truth but for now I am going to let this shit go until I am ready to visit it again. Go to the bathroom and rinse your mouth." Robbie said, "Yes ma'am." And proceeded to go to the bathroom. As he walked by Anthony he touched his head in a fake loving way to show his concern. Grace knocked his hand off of Robbie's head and said, "Don't touch my damn child, I already don't believe this shit, somebody lying, and I am going to find out the truth sooner or later! That just doesn't make any sense!" Anthony looked at her as if he wanted to hit her, he bit his bottom lip and said, "Now you wrong as hell, if you think that I would put my hands on him like that and it's really pissing me off because you know me better than that!" Grace walked up to his face, looked him in the eyes and said, "I don't know you like that! You looking at me like you want to hit me and I got news for you, if you think about putting your damn hands on me I will kill your ass!" Anthony put his finger in her face as if he wanted to push her forehead and he said, "You right, you don't know me like that, but you are not about to talk to me any kind of way and threaten me because you will get to know the side of me that demands respect because I am the king of this castle!" Oh my god, Robbie thought. Did he just say that to Grace?

That was the wrong thing to say because Grace loved Anthony but if he crossed the line she would put him in his place quickly. She was known for fighting men and knocking them out so she wasn't afraid of him and Robbie knew that. She knocked his finger out of her face and she said, "Nigga I don't give a fuck about you thinking you the king, you don't own a damn thing here and if you don't like it you can get the fuck out of his house because I pay the bills and there is no man that is going to come in here and think they are going to run me! We will be two dead ass people in here, so try me!" Anthony was hot as fire, he could not believe that Grace was saying those things to him because he felt like he was the boss and untouchable, so he didn't know how to take everything that Grace was saying to him.

Anthony put on his hat, grabbed his cigarettes looked at her saying, "I don't need this shit from you and you are not going to treat me like this because you mad about your damn son! I didn't do shit to that boy, he told you I didn't, but you want to blame me anyway! This is some bull shit and I am leaving you don't have to worry about me no damn more!" Grace was already on fire and at that point she didn't care about anything that Anthony had to say so she said bye and slammed the door in his face. Robbie could not believe what was happening, but he loved every bit of it because he felt like GOD was answering his prayers. All he needed to do was wait on Him and believe that he would come through just like Miss Suzie said. Anthony stood there in front of the door for a few minutes in disbelief, then stormed out and walked down the street.

Robbie was in the bathroom rinsing his mouth out, when Jake came inside and said, "Why did you do that? Why did you tell a lie?" Robbie didn't know how to respond, he didn't want Jake to think that it was ok to be abused and Grace always taught them to tell the truth rather than lie because lying never ends well. Robbie told him to come all the way inside, so he could close the door and said, "You know that mama love him and you know that she may be mad now but she will be back with him sooner or later. If I would've told her the truth she would have thought that I was making up stuff and confront Anthony, then he would know that I tried to tell everything on him so after he got back on mama good side things would get worse for me!" Jake said, "That's not true, mama would believe you and she would kick him out of the house." Robbie said, "It has to be done the right way, you don't understand now but you will later." Jake just shook his head and left the bathroom, still mad.

Robbie felt bad because he didn't want Jake to be upset, he knew that his little brother looked up to him and he wanted to keep it that way. As he finished up in the bathroom, he stared at his reflection in the mirror for a while, trying to motivate himself to keep going. He heard footsteps in the hallway and noticed Grace standing in the door way, watching him stare into the mirror. He jumped and said, "Mama you scared me!" she smiled and said, "Boy do you know who your mama is and what blood is running through your body?" Robbie said, "Yes ma'am." Grace told him that there shouldn't be a scared bone in his body because he came from her. Robbie responded, "Yes ma'am." There was something about Grace that was very different, and Robbie got chills from hearing her say that to him. She put her hands on her hips, turned her head to the side and asked him what he thought about Anthony. Robbie asked her what she meant by that and she said "Do you think he is a good person? Do you like him? Do you think that I made the right decision by being with him?" It was tough for him to answer her because despite the truth about Anthony, Robbie knew Graced loved him and he didn't want her beating herself up about her choices in men. Robbie wanted Grace to be happy regardless of what he was going through, and he knew Grace's tendency to be hard on herself. If he would have told her the truth, she would hate herself and she would never forgive herself. Robbie had to think about her emotional wellbeing. Robbie paused to gather his thoughts and said "Mama, Anthony is different he is not like any man that you have ever dated, I know you love him, and he makes you happy which is all that matters to me. I don't really know him like that to say that I like him a lot, but I do know that God makes things happen for a reason and you are with him for a reason mama. You are so pretty, and he should be lucky that you gave him a chance but he is ok I guess."

That was as nice as Robbie could put it without throwing up and telling the truth. He told her what he knew she wanted to hear so that she could move away from the subject. She smiled and said, "Son you are very special, different from most kids, but you are strong, and you always know what to say. I know that Anthony can be difficult sometimes, but I do love him, and I thank you for loving me enough to want to see me happy. You never cease to amaze me son." Robbie told her she was welcome, and she turned around and walked back to her room.

CHAPTER
14

There are times in life where it's possible to hurt the people you love most by telling the truth. This was Robbie's line of thinking when he decided to lie to Grace and cover up the abuse he was experiencing. But one thing she was right about was that Robbie was different from everyone and he was stronger mentally than some adults. A lot of people would tell Robbie that he had an old soul. He was also mature because of the trauma he endured on a regular basis. He had a lot of experience and knowledge of things that many children his age didn't. One of his favorite things was having conversations with adults as they expressed amazement at how much he knew. After Robbie finished cleaning in the bathroom, he headed to his room to get ready for bed. He knew that Jake was still upset with him, but Grace always told them to never go to bed mad at each other because anything could happen. Jake was in bed, facing the wall with the covers over his head so Robbie turned on the light prompting him to yell, "Turn the light off!" Robbie calmly replied, "I will when you sit up and talk to me." Jake said, "I don't want to talk to you ever again!" Robbie reminded him that their mother told them never to go to bed mad at each other because one of them could die. Jake angrily replied, "So what! I don't care anymore! You are a chicken! You are scared of him! You lied!" This was really making Robbie upset, but he knew that Jake just needed to calm down and listen to him talk, so he said, "Brother I am so sorry that you think that about me, but I am not a chicken." He took the cover off of his head, sat up, and looked at Robbie, saying, "So why did you take up for him when you know that he wasn't playing? Why did you not tell the truth?" Robbie knew then that he had to be honest with Jake so that he could understand where why he was handling the situation this way.

He put his hand on Jake's shoulder and said, "I am doing this for ya'll, I am doing this, so he won't hurt ya'll or mom! Yeah, he is beating me brother, and I hate it really bad, but I would rather it is me than ya'll!" He seemed shocked to hear Robbie say that, and he began to cry and said

"We have to kill him then brother! We have to figure out a way to make him leave! I hate him he is not my daddy! Let's kill him!" Robbie felt Jake's anger escalate and he knew right then that he meant every word that he said. He would do anything that Robbie told him to do because he was Jake's big brother. But Robbie knew that he had to plan things out strategically plan this out in order for it not to end in death. Robbie responded, "We will kill him without having to touch him." Jake pulled away to look up at him then he said, "What do you mean? I am confused, in order to kill somebody, you have to shoot them, fight them, stab them!" He pulled Jakes head back in and said, "No you don't, we can find a way to make him go away without having to do none of that, just let me figure it out and I promise you that when I know what we are going to do I will tell you." He saw that Jake believed him although he wasn't completely confident about what he'd just told him.

Robbie had no clue what he was going to do, he was afraid of Anthony most of the time, he had already nearly beat him to death. Jake looked at Robbie with a smile and said, "Ok we got this, we will beat him really bad the smart way." Robbie smiled back and said, "Yes we will, I love you brother and I will never let anybody hurt you, our sisters, or mom!" He said, "I know, and I love you too!" It was bed time and he knew that they had to get up early so he suggested something different. Robbie wanted them to say their prayers together because their mother always told them that a family who prays together, stays together. Jake agreed but then he said, "We have to go get mommy and our sisters because we are all a family, right?" Robbie said, "Yes you are right so let's go get them so that we can all pray together." They jumped off the bed and took off to Grace's room screaming, "Mom!!! Mom!! Let's pray together!" These were the moments that Robbie absolutely loved! Happiness was rare in their household so when they got a chance to experience it, they made the best of it!

Grace was laid across the bed, half asleep when the children made it to her room. They startled her a little, but she was smiling when they ran in and jumped on her bed. Robbie was always the leader of the pack no matter what, so he said, "Mom you said that a family who prays together stays together so we all want to pray, and I am going to start off the prayer and we can all go in turns." Laura shouted out, "No, I am the oldest, so I should go first, and I am a girl too and girls are always first." Robbie rolled his eyes and said, "Why are you always trying to mess everything up? Let's just let mama go first!" Laura was always trying to do things her way or no way. This always caused conflict between them because Robbie had the most responsibility, so he always felt like the oldest. Grace was already tired and had to get up early for work, so she said, "Look kids, ya'll better cut that arguing out, I will start the prayer and we will go around in a circle so bow your heads so we can pray!" The children all looked at her and said, "Yes ma'am."

Grace may have been a fighter and partied from time to time but one thing about her was that she loved God! The family went to church every chance that they got when she wasn't working, and Grace made sure that they always had God in their hearts. Robbie was beside her as they all kneeled to pray, Grace grabbed his hand tightly and said, "Dear God, I come to you as humbly as I know how, knowing that you know my thoughts and my wants, my desires, my needs but before I go into detail, I would like to ask for forgiveness of my sins. Lord I have ups and downs just like the rest of people on this earth in this life time, but I come to you to say keep me and my kids strong through these trying times, I want to spend more time with my kids Lord, be able to do things for them, keep them protected Lord, send your anointing right now upon us oh Lord!" Grace was a very powerful woman, so her voice was stern and you would know when she meant something. As she prayed, tears began to run down her eyes, she began to breathe hard and squeeze Robbie's hand until it went numb. Robbie cracked open his eyes to peek at his siblings and they were looking at Grace like they were afraid, not knowing that the presence of God was in the room. They were a family that needed guidance, order, and faith. Grace knew it, so this was the perfect time for her to let go and give it all to God. When she was done praying and she tapped Laura to go but she didn't want to because she had started to cry from seeing Grace cry. It was his baby Tori's turn and she just said, "Thank you Jesus, pray for my family, help my family I love you." Next was Jake's turn and Robbie was shocked that he had nothing to say when earlier he was wide open about praying as a family. When it was Robbie's turn, he felt like this was the moment that he had been waiting for. He wanted to talk to God in front of his family especially Grace and wanted everyone to hear what he had to say. He knew that he was taking too long to start because he saw Grace open her eyes look at him and then pull his hand as if she was prompting him to start praying.

Robbie took a deep breath, opened his eyes, looked at everyone, and closed his eyes to pray. He felt nervous but was ready to speak from his heart. He copied Grace's intro and said, "Lord I come to you as humbly as I know how, I really don't know how to say this Lord because I am nervous, but mama told me that I should talk to you like you are my best friend, so that's how I am going to talk Lord. I am happy right now to have my real family here with me to pray to you God. Our lives haven't been easy because we never get to spend time with mama, but I want you to change that God. When mama is home, we all are very happy because we love her, and she makes us laugh, she is very funny and she protects us from the devil, God. We do have the devil in our family and I want you to take him out of our family because we don't deserve evil and we are not bad people, God. I want you to help me and my siblings in school so that we can all graduate. Please give mama a new job so that she can rest and relax because she works very hard, she doesn't make enough money and it is not right that she has to pay all of the bills. Mr. Anthony doesn't pay anything all he do is sit home and do nothing at all. Can you please get him a job so that he can help her? Mama always told us that a man is supposed to be working and paying the bills and he is not doing that God. Also get him some new clothes and a tooth brush because he always wears the same clothes and his breath stinks really bad." Robbie was really getting into this prayer, he felt like he had to say what was on his mind and he wanted his mother to listen to what really on his mind. Grace needed to know that Robbie felt Anthony was really a sorry excuse for a man. As Robbie said his prayer, the siblings all had grins on their face and they were shocked at the same time because they didn't think that he would have said anything like that. Grace had her eyes wide open, shocked about what Robbie was saying but she let him finish.

Robbie continued on with his prayer, "God can you please get mama a new car because her car is old, and she is really pretty and nice and she is a good mother and she deserves to be riding in a nice car, but she has no help because Mr. Anthony doesn't work. God, I feel good about praying because I know that you will help us, and I know that you will hear his prayer. Mam told us to have faith and I have faith. God you are my best friend in the whole wide world and I want to talk to you every single day. God, I have to go to bed now, but can you protect me, mama, and my siblings, make sure that we are safe and sound? Wherever Mr. Anthony is, can you please tell him to stay there because it's too late for him to be gone so he may as well stay where he at, so the devil can get out of him for good. I am going to bed now in Jesus' name I pray, Amen."

Robbie lifted up his head and Grace was crying, she was rocking back and forth, saying "Lord what have I done, why am I always going through this?" He didn't know what to do because he hated seeing his mother cry, all he wanted her to do was listen to what he had to say, but he didn't mean to make her sad. He was feeling bad about his prayer, and walked over to Grace, putting his hand on her back. He asked her what was wrong and if he had said something wrong. She looked back at him and said, "Thank you so much son, you didn't do anything wrong at all. You actually taught me a lesson and you woke me up. This is exactly what I needed to hear coming from my own child. You are right, I need to be treated like a Queen, Anthony needs to get a job, I need a new car, I need to be treated better and I need to spend more time with my babies." She kissed Robbie on his forehead and told him to go to bed. Robbie was still a little down about making his mother cry but the words he spoke needed to be heard. Anthony was still gone Grace was home alone crying, she deserved better and she knew it. Robbie didn't think she realized how beautiful she was and that she could get any man she wanted. He just wanted his mother happy and was willing to do anything for her to have that. In Robbie's eyes, she was the most loving woman in the world, he noticed that she wore her heart on her sleeve, and men took advantage of it. As he walked toward his bedroom his heart ached because he could still hear her crying and it got worse. He wanted to go back in her room and lay his head on her shoulder until she stopped crying. The later it got into the evening Robbie reasoned that Anthony wouldn't come back home that night. Anthony loved for Grace to be mad at him, because that was his way to get out of the house and not come home. Robbie knew that he was up to no good, and probably with one of his other women. And although he didn't want Anthony with his mother, he didn't want him being unfaithful to her either. Robbie wanted desperately to tell Grace everything, but he knew that she wasn't ready to hear it. Grace would have lost her mind and ended up in jail for murder. He didn't want to lose Grace because of Anthony then he and his siblings would be stuck with him and Robbie would have preferred death than to have that outcome.

Grace loved Anthony to the core so even though she was mad, she wouldn't let him go easily. He had manipulative ways and knew how to get her back to normal which Robbie hated because he knew that Anthony was full of shit. He thought to himself, "Why does she put up with this man? She has to know that he is a sorry ass hole!" That's the thing about love, when you love someone and it's sincere, you can tolerate more. You have more patience and you feel like you don't want to go through finding someone all over again, so you put up with the bull shit until you get fed up. Robbie knew this at a very young age because he'd seen it play out too many times in Grace's other relationships minus the abuse. He'd seen Grace get hurt over and over and he was the one who would hear the crying, feel the hurt, listen in on her arguments and conversations and learn from it. As Grace went through things, he paid attention, he was like a sponge and soaked in everything he saw and heard. When Robbie laid down on his bed he noticed Jake was crying too. Robbie sat up beside him and asked him what was wrong, he said, "I hate when mama cry, I hate Anthony, and I wish he never come back!" Robbie smiled and said, "We all do brother, but you have to keep asking God to fix this for them and Anthony will never come back again because God is stronger than any man." He said ok and laid down to get some rest. Robbie laid back and tried to tune out Grace's crying but nothing he did seemed to drown out the sound of it. She was hurt by life and he knew that the words he spoke during the prayer were really affecting her. He decided that if she kept crying he would go in there with her until she stopped. He waited 10 minutes and as he was getting up to check on Grace there was a knock on the front door. It was pretty late in the evening for Grace to be having visitors. Robbie stood to the edge of the door that led to his room, Grace got herself together, walked to the door and said, "Who is it?" the voice on the other side of the door said, "Tasha, my name is Tasha and I am here to speak to you about Anthony."

CHAPTER
15

G race opened the door and there was this very short lady with a big belly that looked like she was pregnant. Robbie thought to himself, "Now this has got to be Christmas and my birthday all in one day!" Anthony was already in the dog house with Grace and then some random lady shows up while he is away to speak to Grace, he was really loving this day!

Grace looked her up and down, frowned and said, "May I help you?" Tasha said, "Can I come in please?" Grace said, "No my kids are in here trying to sleep, I will come outside." This looked like it was about to get really serious and Robbie didn't want to miss the action! He was getting excited because God was finally answering his prayers.

Grace cracked the door behind her slightly and started to listen to what the lady had to say. Robbie tried to find a way to get close enough so that he could hear what was going on without getting caught listening. He slowly and quietly walked down the hall and snuck into the living room. It was really quiet at first because Tasha was whispering, so he could barely hear what she was saying and suddenly she was crying, and her voice became louder as she spoke. She said to Grace, "This is his baby and I can't believe that he is doing this to me. I didn't find out about you until yesterday when one of his cousins came to me and told me that he had seen him over here a lot, but he told me that he lived in country with his brother. I didn't mean to come over here at this time of night trying to start something, but my feelings are so hurt and that sorry ass Anthony has been lying to me this whole time. I am nineteen years old, we have been together for two years and when I finally got pregnant, I told him about it and he told me that he was going to help me take care of the baby and that everything was going to be ok, but then he stopped coming around and answering my calls. He blamed it on him working and sleeping all of the time but deep down inside I knew that was a lie!" Robbie was surprised but not really shocked because he knew that Anthony was a no-good piece of shit. He was just hurt because Grace loved him, and she allowed him to be in their lives, but he betrayed her. Grace was very quiet as she listened to this strange woman tell her side of the story. Robbie knew that she was super pissed and ready to kill Anthony because whenever was really quiet and it meant she was plotting to go off into a rage. And when Grace was in a rage, it was best for the target of her anger to be as far away from her as possible. The conversation was coming to an end really quickly because Grace was not responding, and Tasha seemed to get the hint that it was time to go.

She said, "I know that you are upset, and I would be too, you don't deserve this, I don't deserve this and we should both confront him whenever you are ready. Grace finally spoke, saying, "Right now I am trying to get my anger together and calm down because I really want to beat his ass but it's not even worth that. You are just a baby and you were seventeen years old when he was dealing with you, which means he is a pedophile!" Suddenly Grace was crying like she had been stabbed in the back, it sounded so painful like she was losing her life and then she said, "Child I am so sorry that you had to go through this I had no idea this whole time, I would have never known any of this, but we will get to the bottom of this ok. You go back home and try to get you some rest and take care of that baby, if he contacts you at any time please give me a call, here is my number and you give me yours as well. I will make sure to give you a call when I find out more."

Tasha was crying too as she walked away. It was all so sad because she was so young, and he basically took advantage of her, when she got to the end of the yard she turned and said, "Thank you so much for not going off on me and listening to everything that I had to say. I will let you know if I hear from him and I won't even tell him anything about what I know or us talking, I will just wait to hear from you so that we can carry out our plan." Grace responded, "Ok sweetie you have a good night." This was Robbie's cue to get to his bedroom as quickly as possible in order to not get caught by Grace. She was already pissed to the point of no return and she probably would have snapped me him in half. He bolted to his room and jumped into his bed to pretend to be asleep. Grace usually came by their rooms to look in on them when she was home during the night.

Robbie laid there in the bed for about fifty minutes and heard nothing, not a word from Grace and this wasn't good. He had to see what was going on and check on her, so he got up and quietly walked to where he could normally hear her. It was dead silence; her door was closed and he couldn't hear anything so he began to panic. His heart was racing, his thoughts were all over the place, Robbie knew that Grace loved this man and she could possibly hurt herself over what she had just heard. Robbie didn't want this to happen, but it was something that was very possible. He didn't want to burst in the room and find Grace laying there unconscious or injured so he decided to act like his stomach was hurting. He walked to the door and screamed, "Mama! Mama! Mama!" she didn't reply so he really began to worry, he knocked on the door and wasn't going to stop until she opened the door, or he was breaking the door down. He called for her and knocked over and over and she never responded so he opened the door and there was Grace sitting beside the bed on the floor with a gun in her hand. She had tears running down her face, her eyes were blood shot red and it looked as if she was in a state of shock.

Robbie could see in Grace's eyes that night that she was about to do something that she would regret, and he couldn't let that happen. He slowly approached her, so nervous that he was shaking. He had never seen Grace like this, so he didn't really know what to do, he sat down beside her and stared at her. She was in another world it seemed, Robbie nervously said "Mama what's wrong, why do you have that gun?" She didn't respond so he reached out to touch her hand and it was like an alarm went off snapping her out of the trance she was in. Suddenly she looked at him and started to apologize over and over saying, "I'm so sorry baby I am so sorry!" She grabbed Robbie and she hugged him tightly crying vigorously rocking back and forth. Robbie could feel the hurt in her heart. He knew that if he hadn't come inside that room that she would have hurt herself or hurt Anthony. Robbie said, "Mama it's ok, everything will be alright please don't hurt yourself." She took cupped Robbie's face with her hands and kissed him on the forehead. Then looked into his eyes and said "Listen to me, you don't ever have to worry about me doing anything to myself, mama isn't going anywhere. I will be ok baby." She wrapped her arms back around him and hugged him again. Robbie didn't truly believe that she wouldn't have hurt herself he knew she was trying to put a positive spin on things to make him feel better.

Grace was good at hiding things especially her emotions and Robbie knew this because he was the same way, so he just played along with what she was saying. It was getting late and Robbie was getting sleepy, so he decided to go back to bed now that he knew Grace was better. He glanced at Grace, she looked so worried and sad, her eyes were baggy, and blood shot red from all of the crying that she was doing, she was shaking because her nerves were bad, and she was rocking back and forth. She didn't deserve this, she had always been a good woman to Anthony. Robbie grabbed her hands and said, "Mama I love you more than anybody in this whole world and I am going to protect you. I don't want you to cry no more, you are really pretty, and you don't have to cry." She smiled, agreed and told him to go to bed. He ran out of the room, jumped in the bed and went to sleep.

The next morning came around fast, Robbie felt so exhausted, due to staying up late worrying about Grace. He heard a noise in Grace's room, which was odd because usually Grace would be gone to work by the time that the children got up for school. He thought to himself that it had to be Anthony, so he must've came home in the middle of the night. This wasn't good because that only meant that she gave him another chance and they would be back to square one and that was hell! Robbie got his siblings up and I started to help them get ready for school. He was in a really bad mood because of Grace giving that asshole another chance. He just knew that this was about to be a bad day, and then the door to Grace's room opened. To his surprise, Grace walked out of the room looking like she had just woken up. He was so relieved, all of the children ran to Grace and surrounded her with hugs and kisses. They were all screaming, "Good morning Mama!" this was like Christmas to see Grace home instead of Anthony.

All of them were wondering, why was Grace home, so Robbie decided to ask her. He got Grace's attention and said, "Mama what are you doing home? I thought you had to work." She responded, "I did have to work baby but I am not feeling well so I took the day off." Robbie knew that she wasn't telling the truth, Grace never took off from work no matter how sick she was. It had to be something to do with all the drama from the previous night. If Grace wasn't working, things were about to get ugly, so he had to prepare for the worst. Grace had decided to make breakfast before the children left for school which she'd never done on a school day. Robbie loved every bit of it. Everyone got dressed for school while Grace cooked breakfast, when Robbie finished he ran to the kitchen table to watch her cook. She seemed so sad and depressed and she was extremely quiet, but

Robbie knew what she was dealing with and figured that she was probably planning what she was going to do about Anthony. He would have usually been home by now, but something told Robbie that either the lady that came over last night had contacted him and he was afraid to come home or he was out being the his usual dirt bag self. It didn't matter either way to Robbie, he was hoping he was lying somewhere dead. Grace finished breakfast and set the table, the children said their grace and started to eat their food.

Everything seemed perfect as it always was whenever Anthony wasn't there, it was like a dream come true and Robbie enjoyed every bit of it! The food was amazing, in Robbie's mind his mother was the greatest cook ever. The children all finished their food and it was time to get to school, Grace grabbed her purse and keys, then walked to the front door and said, "Come on his babies, I am taking ya'll to school today." All of the children got so excited and took off towards the car! Robbie thought he was dreaming, he woke up to his mother being home, they had breakfast and she would be taking them to school! He was thanking God over and over in his head! On the way to school, his siblings were talking Grace to death because they were so happy and enjoying that she was taking them to school. Robbie was in the front seat, as they talked to mother, he just stared at her like he was in love. He truly adored Grace she was his hero no matter what they had been through, he knew there was nobody on this planet that could love him the way that Grace loved him. She calmed his soul, made him feel secure, happy and she didn't have to do anything but be around. He was worried about what was going to happen when Anthony came home, but whatever happened he was going to be right by Grace's side ready to fight and kill.

When the children had got to school, Grace gave them all kisses and told them that she would see them later. As Robbie was closing the door, he looked at Grace and said, "Mama everything will be ok, just pray and God got you." She smiled and said, "I know baby, I know." Then she drove off and Robbie walked into school. This was one of those days that he just wanted to be with his mother. He wasn't feeling like going to school at all. He was already anticipating a big blow up and felt like he needed to be near Grace in order to protect her. Robbie would die or kill for Grace, and he was willing to do whatever it would take to safe. The whole day at school, he could only concentrate on getting his mind right to be ready to fight Anthony.

The last period bell rang, and it was time to leave school, Robbie hoped that Grace would be there to pick him up but he knew that if she hadn't come by the time he started walking, he would need to carry on with the normal routine. He grabbed his book bag headed on his normal route when he got about 15 minutes into his walk he heard a voice scream, "Hey boy come here I need to talk to you!" He didn't turn around, but he knew that voice so well, it was Anthony! Robbie felt his heart drop. He never believed that anybody his age could have a heart attack, but he felt like this was 'the big one' like Fred Sanford would say. Anthony kept screaming his name over and over and he kept walking faster. He could not let him know that he heard him, so he ignored him and sped up his pace. There was a train coming and he knew that if he made it across the tracks that he could vanish without him knowing where he was but if he got caught by the train, Anthony would have gotten to him and there was no telling what would have happened. Robbie heard his voice getting closer and he heard Anthony say "I know your little punk ass hear me! Come here boy!"

There was no way that Robbie was about to let himself be caught so he sprinted across the tracks so that he could beat the train and when he made it across he looked back and could see Anthony waiting for the train to end. This was his time to take off, Robbie sprinted like he was running in the Olympics he had to get away from Anthony so he ran through people's yards and took a different way to get home until he felt confident he had lost him. He made it to the side of an abandoned house and waited to see if Anthony was still on his trail. He waited for thirty minutes and there was no Anthony, but he knew that he had to be careful.

Robbie was on guard as he walked to his siblings' school to pick them up, there was no sign of Anthony which was great. He told them all that they had to get home fast, but they would be going a different way. Robbie and his siblings went almost an hour out of their way to get home, but they finally made it. They were all exhausted until they saw Grace's car in the yard. They were all so happy that she was home they got an instant burst of energy. When they got inside the house it was very quiet, their mother was asleep on the couch. She jumped up as if her alarm clock went off and she looked around disoriented. Robbie approached her saying, "Hey mama! I missed you!" She kissed him on his forehead and said, "Hey son, how was school?" He responded, "It was ok until after school." Her face went from a smile to a look of concern and her head slightly turned to the side as she said, "What happened after school?" Robbie was nervous but knew that he needed to tell her considering the situation with her and Anthony. He took her hands and said, "Well when I was walking home from school, I heard this voice and it was Mr. Anthony, and he was calling me to come talk to him and I acted like I didn't hear him and I kept walking and he got mad and he cussed at me and told me to come talk to him but I saw the train coming, I hurried up and got across the track, then I took off running so he couldn't find out where I had gone."

Robbie could tell that Grace was upset, he could see every frown in her face even the ones he never knew she had. She stood up and put her hands on her hips said, "That bitch ass motherfucker! He got the nerve to cuss at my child and his ass has not even been home! I am so sorry that you had to deal with that baby, mama will handle it." Robbie loved the fact that Grace was so mad at Anthony because he deserved it. He thought about telling Grace even more, but he didn't want to push her over the edge emotionally, so I decided not to. Robbie replied, "Ok mama." They went to their rooms to do their homework. Grace was so angry that she looked like a female lion wanting to protect cubs, she looked like she wanted to kill. Robbie was waiting on Anthony to walk in the house like he normally did when he had been out all night. Usually Grace never harassed him or asked him anything and he walked in and out like nothing was supposed to be said to him. This time was going to be different Grace didn't play any games when it came to her children, so Robbie could not wait to see how everything was going to happen. Robbie had to help his siblings with their homework as well as get his done. He took all of his responsibilities seriously because he knew that Grace expected him to make sure that everything was taken care of.

As the children finished up their daily routine Grace rattling and mumbling words of anger about what happened. It sounded like she was getting herself amped up for the moment that Anthony walked through the door. She was pacing the living room, looking out the window, cleaning up things that were already cleaned, moving things that didn't need to be moved, and it was beginning to make them all nervous because they had never seen Grace that angry. Anthony's best bet was to stay away from Grace because Robbie knew things would get violent this time. Robbie decided to try to lighten the mood because the atmosphere was tense and uncomfortable, so he asked Grace if they could all watch a movie together since everything was done. Robbie wanted to get her mind back to normal and off of Anthony. The children all sat down on the couch and waited for Grace to come and sit with them, the movie that they decided on was "The Terminator", it was one of their favorites and Grace loved it as well. Once Grace joined the children they all loved on her because they knew she needed it, it was one of the best moments and it worked. She calmed down completely and was even laughing at certain parts of the movie. This was an awesome feeling, to have her in such a good mood after what had taken place.

The movie ended, the children ate dinner and got ready for bed. The night was still young, but it came to an end on a great note and Robbie felt satisfied with the outcome. Anthony was still missing in action. There was no abuse, nobody staring at them with mean looks, no fake love, and it was all family like it was supposed to be. Things felt too good to be true, Robbie had a feeling in his gut that something was about to happen to change his mood, but he tried to stay positive for as long as he could. The children put on their pajamas, brushed their teeth, and went to their mother's room for prayer again. As they walked into her room, they heard her crying and she was sitting on the edge of the bed with her hands on her face. Robbie knew the reason for her crying had to be something dealing with that demon man, even though she was pissed at him, he had a hold on her that she just couldn't seem to escape.

The children all hugged Grace and told her not to cry. Grace loved hard, so it affected her in a major way that Anthony was doing these things and it upset Robbie with everything in his soul. She told them to go to bed and that she would be ok, and Robbie just wanted to go to bed. He was worn out from the stress of it all. The children went to their rooms and got into bed. Robbie closed his eyes and tried to get some rest but couldn't, his mind was racing with thoughts of Anthony coming back, and how he would treat him whenever Grace left them alone with him. Robbie knew that Anthony would try his best to destroy him because he was sure that when Grace finally saw him that she would mention to him what happened the day he was calling his name and Robbie ran from him. He knew that would put him into a secret rage once he found out that Grace knew, and Robbie would be headed for a long session of abuse. He thought to himself, "What are you going to do? Will you accept it? Will you fight back? Will you tell on him?" He was unsure about all of it, he was just tired and fed up with everything in life concerning this man, he has been nothing but negativity towards them all in every way, he hurt their family, and something had to be done to stop him.

Robbie felt like he couldn't get through to Grace, she was in too deep, no matter what he said to her. He knew she wouldn't let Anthony go and she would find a way to make it ok just as long as he was around. Nobody understood how the possibility of him coming back impacted Robbie, because he was the one being tortured. Anthony hated Robbie, he was a threat to him because Grace made Robbie the man of the house before Anthony was even involved with her. It seemed as though no matter what this man had done to Grace she still viewed him as her king. Robbie decided to just give it to God and let Him keep the family safe and protected.

That night felt different than any other, Robbie just needed to close his eyes and wake up with a new attitude. He stared at the wall until he eventually dozed off into a restless sleep where he began to dream. In the dream, Robbie was walking down a dirt road, there were big trees, and it was dark and spooky looking. He looked around, trying to figure out where he was, and he could hear Grace calling his name so he started to follow her voice. He could not see her, so he felt himself beginning to panic because all he could see were trees and darkness. His heart was racing, Grace was still calling his name and he started to run but suddenly he saw dark clouds forming. Those clouds grew darker and started to swirl as if a tornado was forming, the wind was blowing hard and the trees swaying bending from the force of it. Through the wind, he could still hear Grace's voice, but the winds were blowing him backwards stopping him from getting any closer to Grace. Then he heard an evil laugh and it sounded like Anthony, Robbie was being blown all over the place, every time that he got up he was knocked right back down. Anthony's voice was getting closer and Robbie was running as fast as he could to try to get away from him and make it to Grace. Suddenly the wind stopped, and everything was calm, but Robbie was still far away from her and it was becoming more and more upsetting. He began to scream for her, asking where she

71

was, he could still hear her voice, then it stopped. He looked around and to his surprise the dirt road and darkness turned into a church filled with a lot of people who he recognized to be his family members. There was a casket at the front of the church, it was a funeral! Robbie walked towards the casket, as he walked he saw his five aunts, four uncles, and all of his cousins. They were all crying, looking sad and passing out all over the place as if someone very important was dead. Robbie's heart thumped in his chest, so he started running towards the casket when he suddenly stopped. When he stopped running it was like he was no longer in his body, he saw himself dressed in a black suit, standing over the casket crying. But it was like he didn't really exist, nobody could see him. Robbie slowly walked up to the casket to see why he was crying, he was getting more nervous about seeing who it was, so he put his hands over his eyes. Suddenly Anthony appeared and snatched Robbie's hands off of his eyes and said, "Look what you have done! This is your fault! You are next! I am going to kill you too!" It was Grace in the casket! His heart dropped, and he screamed but nobody could hear him but Anthony. He grabbed Robbie by his neck and began to choke him. Robbie was trying his best to fight back but he couldn't. All he could say was, "Mama, help!" Anthony was laughing and said, "That Bitch can't hear you she is dead!" Robbie grabbed Anthony's hands and tried to move them away from his neck, screaming, "No, my mama is not dead you are!" All of a sudden, a gunshot went off and Anthony disappeared! Robbie was laying on the ground gasping for air. He heard Grace's voice again then he got up and ran towards her, he could see her smiling. Robbie reached out for her and touched her hand, then he woke up and touching Jake's hand. Jake yelled at him, "Get off of me I am going to tell mama!"

Robbie jumped up and looked around, his body was drenched in sweat, and shuddered. He needed to find Grace A.S.A.P.! He got up and ran towards Grace's room screaming "Mama! Mama! Mama!" He had frightened her, she came flying out the room, her eyes wild with panic, she said, "Boy what's wrong with you?" Robbie said, "Mama, you died in my dream, Anthony killed you Mama!" She looked at him sternly as if she was signaling him not say his name and she said, "Go back to bed son, nobody is killing your mama ok." Robbie looked at her and said, "Mama what's wrong?" She gave him the look again and told him to go back to bed. He stood there because he knew Grace and there was something she wasn't saying so he said, "Mama, can I sleep with you? I am very afraid I had a bad dream!" She frowned and said, "No boy now go back to bed before I whoop your butt!" As Robbie slowly turned to walk back to his room he heard Anthony's voice and it stopped him in his tracks.

Anthony said, "Hey son, come here for a minute please." Robbie was in disbelief, he thought he had to have still been dreaming. He didn't want to believe that Anthony was back in the home, he didn't want to accept it. Robbie slowly turned around, hoping and wishing that he was still dreaming, and that Anthony would disappear, but this was a reality not a dream. Anthony was standing in front of Grace's bedroom. He said, "Please son, I am not going to harm you, there is something that I have to say to you." Robbie's heart was breaking, he was so disappointed in Grace and she knew it because she couldn't even look at him, she was so wrong.

Grace knew that Anthony should not have been back in the house, but she showed how weak she was, and it was obvious to everyone but her that Anthony was her weakness. Robbie had just experienced the worst dream of his life, and then woke up to this. Grace had taken this man back into her life after all that he had done. Robbie felt torn apart. As he walked towards Anthony, tears began to run down his eyes, he knew that whatever this piece of shit was about to say was just an act! Anthony was a con artist, he knew exactly what to do to get Grace back and to keep her. Robbie stood with his head down, Grace was standing behind him waiting and watching to see what Anthony was going to say. He was staring at Robbie, but he refused to look up at him. Robbie wished Anthony was dead. The craziest part about this whole situation to Robbie despite all of the abuse Anthony knew he had inflicted on him, here he was pretending to want to talk as if nothing ever happened. He put his hand on Robbie's shoulder to which Robbie responded by quickly stepping back to throw his hand off of him. Grace then came in defense of Anthony and snatched Robbie around roughly as if she could have taken his arm out of the socket. She got up in Robbie's face and said, "Boy have you lost your damn mind? Don't you ever do that again do you understand?" Robbie was so angry at her that he didn't care if he got a beating. He felt betrayed, his heart was broken, and he had lost hope. Grace could have done anything to him physically at that point and it would not have mattered. Robbie felt that if he was going to go out, he might as well go out with a bang.

Robbie remained silent and didn't say word in response to Grace's question. This made her angrier. She took her hand and raised it as if she was about to strike him in the face then Anthony stopped her by saying, "Baby it's ok, he is upset, and I totally understand it, I would be too. I should have never talked to him the way I did that day and I was wrong. I was way out of character, stressed out from me and your situation that I took it out on him and that should have never happened, if I was him I would be very mad too." This act that Anthony was performing was worthy of an Oscar award. Robbie knew he was acting and everything that he said to him went in one ear and out the other. Anthony wasn't fooling him at all, maybe Grace but sure as hell not Robbie. Grace looked at Anthony and broke down crying from the performance. She ate it up, Anthony knew exactly what to say to win her heart over again like he didn't have it in the first place.

Anthony was like an evil genius. He put on this act as a way to get back in, so he could get back to abusing Robbie. Anthony hugged Grace as she cried, but Robbie stood angrily. Robbie decided hen that he didn't care what happened to him anymore, so he was going to act up on purpose. Robbie defiantly stood in front of Grace so hat Anthony could not get to her and he refused to move. Anthony gave him a look as if to signal that he was going to hurt him later, then asked him to step aside. Robbie ignored him and turned around to hug and squeeze her. He knew Anthony was full of shit and it would upset him to see Grace hugging him. Robbie was blocking him from hugging her since he wanted to put on a show, Robbie decided to do the same thing. He knew Anthony hated to see Grace love on her son.

Robbie could feel Anthony's eyes staring at him and he knew that he was livid. Robbie knew just what to do to get on his nerves. Anthony wasn't the only one that knew how to win Grace over. She looked at Robbie and said, "Baby we have to do better, we have to forgive each other even when we know things that were done are wrong. I want you to forgive your step dad just like I did, everybody makes mistakes son we are not perfect. I love all of ya'll and I just want my family to be happy. Can you please forgive him?" Robbie and Anthony exchanged looks of disgust that either

Grace didn't notice, or she ignored. They both knew that when it was all said and done that things would be back to the regular routine. Anthony would do everything in his power to hurt Robbie and Robbie would have to put up with it in order to protect Grace. Robbie never wanted to hurt her because he knew that she loved them both. But he also knew that she would have to find out for herself what kind of monster that this man was. It was only a matter of time before she would find out and Robbie felt that it was coming soon. Until then Robbie decided to do what I had to do to survive and keep the peace. He looked back at Grace and said, "Yes mama I forgive him." She smiled and looked at Anthony, he was frowning at first but quickly smiled back at Grace when he noticed her looking his way. She asked him to come and get a hug. Robbie didn't want to be a part of a group hug, there was no way that he wanted to be anywhere near Anthony, let alone touching him! Robbie quickly got out of the way so that he and Grace could hug but Grace grabbed his head and said, "No Son you don't have to leave, that's your step dad, I really want ya'll to be close. That would make me so happy." Robbie didn't want to hear it, and each time she called Anthony his stepdad, his stomach turned. She wanted them all to hug so Robbie would give her what she wanted. Anthony came into to hug Grace, he raised his other hand up and looked at Robbie to invite him in. Robbie obliged as he reached around quickly and barely touched him during the hug. This was an emotional experience for Grace and it was just another opportunity for Anthony to show his acting skills. Somehow Anthony managed to make tears roll down his face.

Anthony knew that once Grace saw him crying that she would think that this moment meant the world to him and that's exactly what he wanted her to think. Robbie could not believe this was happening and didn't want to be a part of this fake scene. He tried to pull away from them and every time he tried Anthony would bring him in closer and dug into his back with his nails to signal what was coming. He was squeezing Robbie so tight it was as if he was trying to suffocate him. Robbie struggled to breathe as Anthony's clothes smelled like a mixture of musty arm pits, cigarettes and cheap cologne.

Grace and Anthony were kissing each other, going back and forth with compliments. Finally, they released Robbie and he could breathe again, Grace told him that he could go to his room and he sighed with relief. As much as Robbie hated his room, this was one of the times where he really wanted to be there, and he had plans on staying in there until it was time for me to go to school. Robbie thought as he laid down, they would never really be a family as long as Anthony was a part of their lives.

CHAPTER
17

Grace was blindly in love and seemed as if she wanted to stay that way. It was like he was the only man on earth and that she had to be with him no matter what he had done. In her eyes, Anthony was perfect. It was getting harder for Robbie to feel sorry for her because she was choosing this situation and all the hurt that came along with it. He was so disappointed in her and just didn't understand why he could see that Anthony was a con artist and Grace couldn't.

Grace used to be hardcore when it came to men, yeah, she loved hard and knew how to love but she never let it get the best of her like she was doing with Anthony. She would cut a man off with the quickness if she had an issue with him and not think twice about it. Even though this was a good thing to me it was bad to her in the long run because it eventually made her too soft. She had been desperate at the time that she met Anthony. Before him, it had been so long since she had been involved with someone that when he came into the picture she jumped in heart first. She was vulnerable then, and he knew that, so he told her everything that she wanted to hear to get everything and anything that he wanted from her. He knew that she blamed herself for all her failed relationships he convinced her that she was too hard on her exes and that she needed to soften up if she wanted to have a man in her life. He knew all of her weaknesses and he used every one of them against her. He took advantage of Grace's heart and infected her soul.

All Robbie could do was pray to God that he could make it through it all. He felt as though they were all headed towards a tragic ending. And he thought back to this dream, trying to understand it all. He had never felt so hopeless, he had never had a dream as vivid. He wondered if God coming to him through his dreams to try to tell him something. Robbie was so confused and just wanted something to hope for. The more he thought about it, the more it stressed him out. He didn't deserve to be punished this way, and he deep down he knew that. But he also knew that he was a mean kid and didn't like to play with other kids, he loved to fight and was very aggressive. Was this the reason that he was being abused or was the abuse the reason for him acting this way? Robbie didn't know, and he was mad at himself that he didn't feel like a normal kid. He thought there was something wrong with him and maybe he did deserve what was happening to him. He couldn't wait to go to school so that he could get away from that monster.

Jake came in looking sad, Robbie asked him what was wrong. He pointed towards Grace's room and said, "Why is he back? Mommy said that he would be gone forever she lied!" Tears started to run down his face, he was hurt because he knew what Anthony was all about. Jake felt the negativity when Anthony was around, he heard and saw what Anthony did to Robbie and he didn't like it. Robbie thought about how he would answer Jake's questions without making him more upset with their mother. He was too young to understand the grown-up explanation, so Robbie knew he needed to baby the explanation for him. He looked at Jake and said, "Do you love mother?" He looked with a puzzled expression and said, "Yes I love mommy, you know that!" Robbie said, "If mother made you mad, would you be mad at her forever?" He said, "No I can't be mad at mommy forever that's not nice and she is my mommy!" Robbie explained, "Well, mother loves Anthony just like you love her and even though he made her mad she couldn't be mad at him forever just like you wouldn't be mad at her forever if she made you mad. This is why Anthony is back." He frowned and said, "Mommy shouldn't forgive him, she should stay mad at him forever because he is mean, and I don't want him here with us anymore!" He was finally seeing it from Robbie's perspective, before he was 'Team Anthony' he had wanted to give him a chance and let Robbie continue to be abused but now he was fed up and hated him as much as Robbie did. Robbie grabbed the back of Jake's head, bringing their foreheads together and said, "We have to do something to make him go away forever, I will figure out a plan but until then, you keep acting normal because I don't want him to hurt you like he hurts me. He shook his head and said, "No brother I don't like when he hurt you and I will fight him, I will kill him!" He was a bit loud and Robbie didn't want him to be heard so he put his hand over Jake's mouth and whispered, "You need to be quiet because if he or mother hears you then you will get in trouble so calm down everything will be ok." Jake was a stubborn kid with a quick temper and when he got really upset he didn't care what happened to him. This was one of the moments that he didn't care, and Robbie couldn't get him to listen, so he shouted loudly, "I don't care, I don't care I want him to leave now! Why can't we just tell mommy what he did?" Robbie was beginning to panic because he knew that if their mother heard them she would punish them both. So, he had to think of a way to shut Jake up. The only thing he could think of was to make Grace think that he was fighting with Jake. That way only Robbie would get into trouble and not the two of them. Robbie knew he would probably get a beating, but he didn't care.

Robbie didn't have much time to ponder this idea because he heard Grace yell, "What in the hell are ya'll doing in there? Bring your asses here right now!" Jake looked at Robbie and said, "I am going to tell mommy what he did to you and you will just have to be mad at me!" Robbie wasn't ready to let that happen, so he knew he had to hurt Jake to create a distraction. Grace screamed again, "Don't make me come in there! Bring your asses here right now dammit!" Robbie grabbed Jake's arm and yanked him roughly, away from the door. He screamed, "Stop you are hurting me! Stop hurting me!" He heard Grace's heavy footsteps walking towards the room, she was stomping, and Robbie knew she was angry. Robbie also knew that Jake wouldn't understand his reason for hurting him and be mad at him. But he did it anyway, which was his way of protecting Jake from their mother's wrath. Robbie punched Jake in the stomach hard, it caught him so off guard that he lost his breath and was gasping for air. He couldn't allow Jake to say a word once Grace made it to the room. Robbie hit him in his stomach again and started choking him. He could hear Grace getting close, the time had come, and Grace burst into the room to see Robbie hurting Jake. She snatched Robbie off of him and threw him towards the door. With fire in her eyes she looked at him and said, "What the fuck are you doing to my child! That's your brother you don't fight your brother! What happened dammit?" Robbie didn't say anything because he wanted her to focus on him, not Jake. She picked Robbie up by his shirt and held him up against the wall saying, "Do you hear me talking to you? What happened?" Jake was still gasping for air and crying so Robbie knew that he wouldn't say anything. Robbie responded to grace saying, "I was trying to get some sleep and he wouldn't shut up, he made me mad and I hit him!" Grace threw him down on the ground and started to hit Robbie with her hands. As she hit him she was angrily saying, "Oh you think you grown huh? You think you run shit in his house? You want to put your hands on my damn child because he won't let you sleep?" Grace was heavy handed, so her hits were like being hit by a freight truck over and over again.

For some reason Robbie was enjoying this beating but the thought of enjoying being hurt alarmed him. He thought to himself about why he would enjoy such a thing. Grace kept hitting Robbie and screaming at him, "Don't you ever put your fucking hands on my child again do you hear me?" Robbie shuddered and felt chills throughout his body, he wanted the pain, and craved it! Every time she struck him, he smiled. She beat him until she got tired and needed to stop and catch her breath. But it made her even angrier that Robbie wasn't crying and didn't seem to be phased by the beating. A normal kid couldn't take one lick from Grace, but what Grace didn't know was that Robbie was used to being abused, he was building an immunity to physical pain. She didn't know that he had been training his mind to enjoy the pain so that he could tolerate the abuse he was suffering from Anthony. She looked at Robbie as she grasped for air and said, "Oh you think this shit is funny huh? You want to be a man right, well I will beat your ass like a man because none of my kids will ever disrespect me!" She told Jake to get out of the room and he slowly walked to the door with a look in his eyes that seemed as if he'd figured out why Robbie had done this. Grace looked at Jake impatiently because he was moving so slow. She screamed at him, "Get the fuck out of the room! He over here beating your ass and choking you and you want to act like you don't want me to whoop his ass what is wrong with you damn kids?" Grace was livid as Robbie stood quietly, waiting for her to continue to hit him. Jake didn't leave the room and Grace looked frustrated enough to kill them both.

Anthony walked into the room, looked at Grace and said, "Baby we will deal with this later, you are going to hurt that boy if you continue and we definitely don't need that." Robbie glared angrily at Anthony and thought to himself about the fact that he had beaten him much worse than Grace ever could. He understood why Anthony was playing the "good stepdad" role, he was trying to bait Grace into being ok with him beating Robbie, so she wouldn't have to do it. Anthony took Grace by the hand

and said, "We will talk about how to deal with him later maybe it's time for me to stay on him since he wants to laugh at you." Robbie knew this was coming, he was beginning to understand the way that Anthony's devious mind worked. Grace started to walk out of the room but turned to Robbie and said, "It is not over son, oh I am going to handle your ass and I mean it now go to bed and I don't want to hear one sound from you!" Then she said to Jake, "Since you want to protect him after he whooped your little ass then how about you go to bed too, and don't you say shit to me!" This is what Anthony wanted to happen because he now had the upper hand on them, he knew that Grace was upset and all he needed to do now was to get her to agree to him disciplining her children. Robbie got into bed and closed his eyes, knowing that he had a lot to mentally prepare for.

Robbie knew that the worst was yet to come, he was upset with himself because he had shown too much strength. This meant that when it was Anthony's turn to beat him, he would try to kill him since he saw that Grace's beating didn't have any impact. Jake laid down on his bed as well. Robbie felt bad for what he had done to him, but he hoped Jake had figured out why he did it. He wanted to apologize even though Grace told them not to say a word. Robbie whispered to Jake, "Hey, I am sorry for hitting you I didn't want you to tell mother about Anthony, so I had to stop you and I am sorry." At first, Jake didn't say anything, and but he knew that he had heard him. Finally, after about three minutes of silence Jake whispered, "Hey, I know and I am sorry too, I was just mad and I wish I wouldn't have made you get a whooping." Robbie smiled, feeling relieved. He whispered back, "It's ok, you are my little brother and I love you forever. I have to protect you from him and anybody else. We will figure out how to deal with Anthony but until then just get some rest brother." He said ok and then he went to sleep. Robbie wasn't able to fall asleep immediately. His mind was so heavy and full of thoughts, wondering how his mother felt about him smiling while she was disciplining him.

Robbie's intentions were never to make his mother feel disrespected. The smiling almost felt like a reflex for him. He was just so used to being beaten that he craved the pain, it felt good. Robbie even laughed because instead of the hits hurting, they tickled. Robbie felt as though he was changing, turning into a monster. It seemed like sooner or later he would take his anger and use it as a weapon. Whether he would use it a good weapon or a bad one, he didn't know. He wondered if he would take his anger out on someone or something that didn't deserve it. The thought frightened him, and he tried to tell himself that it was temporary and he had the power to turn his anger on and off if need be.

After pondering all of these things, Robbie finally drifted into a restless sleep and began to dream. In the dream, he was sitting on the front porch reading a book that had red cars in it. He heard a noise in the house that sounded like a gunshot and then he heard Grace scream. Robbie threw the book on the ground, jumped up to try to get inside the house. He was running as fast as he could to get to the door but for some reason he was unable to get any closer. He heard more gun shots as Grace screamed. Robbie's heart pounded, and he screamed for Grace, "Mother! Where are you? I am coming, hold on!" She never responded, all she did was scream and the same sound of a gunshot. Robbie stopped and looked around to find another way to get into the house where Grace was. He turned away from the door and saw the book with the red cars glowing and the pages flipping, and it started to move. He followed the book, as he got closer to it, the further away it moved. Robbie continued to follow, the book took him around to the side of the house, and to the back window. Finally, the book allowed Robbie to grab it and as soon as it touched his hands, Robbie was inside the house and in a closet. He was confused about how he'd ended up in the closet, but he recognized it even in the pitch darkness. As soon as Robbie put the book down he heard the gunshot again and Grace' scream. Suddenly there was a light on the outside of the closet and he heard Grace and Anthony arguing. Grace was saying, "Go ahead kill yourself you deserve to die!" Anthony replied, "No bitch I am going to kill you and your kids!" Robbie tried his best to get out and help when heard them wrestling and fighting each other and then it stopped, the light went away. It was dead silence. The closet door opened, and Grace was sitting on the bed reading the book with the red cars in it. She was smiling and very happy, Anthony gone. Robbie walked over to sit down beside Grace as she read the book. She had just been screaming for her life but now she was sitting on the bed smiling as if nothing had happened. This book seemed to have had magical powers because it made Grace light up and she seemed happy. The book had also led Robbie to a way inside the house. He watched as Grace flipped through the pages, she was fascinated by the red cars, every time she flipped a page her face would light up and she smiled. Then he heard footsteps coming down the hall and they were getting louder and louder, closer and closer. Robbie didn't know who was coming but suddenly, Grace stopped and looked up, but her smile had turned into frown. She said to Robbie, "Get behind me and don't worry I won't let anything happen to you!" Robbie grabbed her hand tightly and said, "Ok mother but what's wrong?" She stood in front of him and turned her back towards him clinching her hands into tight fists as if she was getting ready to fight. Suddenly the footsteps stopped, and he knew the person was inside the room although he couldn't see who it was. Each time Robbie tried to move to see, Grace stood in front of him, blocking his view so that nothing could get to him. Then he woke up, shaking and his heart was racing. Robbie looked over at Jake who was sleeping soundly.

Robbie sat up in bed for a while, taking deep breaths to slow his heart rate down. He couldn't relax enough to get back to sleep so he laid there until it was time to get up for school. He was tired of having these crazy dreams. It was pouring rain outside so hard that he could hear the thunder roar, the wind blowing, and he saw the flashes from lightning striking. He heard a noise coming from Grace's room, it sounded like they were arguing again, so Robbie got up to get closer and hear what was going on. He felt confident that the chaos would eventually come to an end. Anthony didn't belong with Grace and it would only be a matter of time until he upset her again.

Robbie snuck out into the hallway, walking as lightly as possible towards Grace's room as if he was a ninja. The closer he got, the more he could hear them going back and forth with the arguing. The storm outside was still going, full force, he heard the thunder booming outside. He still couldn't make out what was being said in the argument, so he moved closer to the door. Eventually he got brave enough to sit right outside the door to listen to the show down. It sounded like Grace was crying as she said, "You are so sorry, how could you get another bitch pregnant and you are supposed to be with me? How?" It was quiet for about two minutes and then Anthony replied, "Now I told you that wasn't my child and I am not seeing the damn girl she is crazy, yes I used to date her, but I have not been with her since I have been with you baby!" Robbie knew he was lying, he'd even been with Grace's best friend, he didn't believe Anthony's denial about the pregnant lady. Grace asked him, "Why would this girl come all the way to my damn doorstep so that she could let me know the truth about you and her? If she was lying do you think the bitch would be crazy enough to come to my house and tell me that my motherfucking man was messing with her and got her pregnant? No nigga! She is not lying, and you know this! I believe her for some reason, but I swear I hope that I am wrong!" Anthony threw something across the room in anger and said, "I told you that wasn't my damn baby, you either believe me or you don't but I am not about to go back and forth about this with you at all! I thought that we were done with that but evidently, we are not! So, if you got something to say go ahead and get this shit out of the way because after tonight I am not going to hear this shit again!" I could not believe that this piece of shit talked to Grace like that and she just allowed him too. Robbie had stood up expectantly when he heard Anthony throw something because he was ready to burst into the room if he thought Anthony was preparing to hit his mother. It wasn't like Grace not to respond to someone talking to her that way. Robbie was prepared to die that night if Anthony had thrown something at his mother.

He reached for the door knob when he heard Grace shout, "Motherfucker don't you ever throw shit in his house, that's my dead mother's jewelry box that you just broke I should fuck you up in this house tonight! Anthony replied, "Are you threatening me? Is that a threat?" Grace replied, "It's a motherfucking promise nigga! I don't give a fuck who you think you are, but you better get the fuck out of my face because I am not the one! You may have beaten your exes and made them scared of you, but you are not about to do that shit to me because I will kill your ass up in here and that's a promise nigga! My mother gave me this before she died, and you want to throw it like it isn't shit because your lying ass is mad about some random bitch showing up at my house telling on your sorry ass! Nigga you have lost your fucking mind, don't throw shit else in his house and I mean that!" Anthony replied, "Baby I apologize, I didn't mean to disrespect you like that, I just got a little angry and I need to work on my temper, that won't happen again."

Anthony was good at manipulating Grace but this time he wasn't good enough. He had thrown the jewelry box that she cherished. It was one of the last things that she had to remember her mother by who had died a couple of years before. Grace's responded to Anthony saying, "Don't call me your baby, your, wife, or nothing until we get this shit under control with you and this bitch, and if you have any other bitches that you have to tell me about then you better tell me now because after this night here I am not putting up with your shit anymore! I am trying to give you the benefit of the doubt because I love you and I really want to be with you, so tomorrow we will call this girl up, tell her to come over and have a face to face conversation with us to see who is telling the truth. I tried to give you a chance to tell me the truth. I want to talk to her together with you and see why she is pinning this unborn child on you." Anthony replied, "Ok look we don't have to do all that, I will tell you the truth so just listen and please don't get mad." Robbie figured he must not want to go through with meeting with the pregnant lady because he was lying about it. He had a feeling that things were about to escalate, and he tried to mentally prepare to be ready to fight for Grace. Grace said, "I knew your ass was lying to me nigga, I felt it in my soul, now go ahead and say what you have to say!" Anthony walked away from her then Grace responded, "No Anthony come back over hear and sit on the bed and look me in my fucking face while you tell me everything." Anthony replied, "Ok but don't be putting your hands on me because I am not trying to go to jail." Grace replied, "Let me tell you something first of all I am a real woman, I am far from a punk, if my fucking man tells me something that I knew he was lying about was true and it's concerning another bitch I am going to react however the hell that I want to nigga so if you feel like you have to react back then do what you have to do, but you are going to sit your ass right here and tell me the truth right now!" Anthony walked back towards Grace and sat on the bed. Robbie's heart was beating fast and his hands were shaking in anticipation. He didn't know what was about to go down, but he knew his mother wasn't afraid of anybody. He also knew that she would fight anybody at any time with no hesitation. Anthony was afraid. Robbie could hear him breathing hard which made him happy because he always tried to act like a big tough guy around him. Grace said, "What are you waiting on? Go ahead and say what you have to say!" Anthony replied, "Ok, I have not been honest with you, me and her have been sleeping together and yes, it is probably my child that she is having. I don't know how else to say this to you, but you have been acting different." He went on to try to say something else and all Robbie heard the sound of a loud smack and Anthony fell to the floor.

Anthony yelled, "Baby why did you do that? Why did you hit me? I told you that I didn't want to go to jail." Grace replied, "You lying son of a bitch, I hate you. How could you do this to me after everything that we have been through! Go ahead hit me nigga and let's go to jail together or the morgue because somebody will die up in this motherfucker tonight if you put your damn hands on me nigga!" Robbie was completely shocked, he finally told her the truth about something but the only reason he did that was because he didn't want to meet up with the girl. Grace broke down crying and she screamed, "I hate you, how could you do this to me? How could you do this to me?" Anthony kept saying that he was sorry over and over again. This was enough for Robbie, he'd heard enough and knew that sooner or later it would be time for him to get up and go to school. He snuck back to his room and got into bed, still shocked at what had just happened. He didn't feel relieved though because he wasn't convinced that Grace would be done with Anthony. She had taken so much from him already, but nothing ever seemed like enough to completely get him out of their lives. Robbie said a quick prayer and decided to let accept whatever was coming next.

CHAPTER 18

Time came passed so quickly from the time that Robbie laid down that it was soon time to get up for school. Grace was up and in the living room quiet as a mouse, Robbie went and sat down beside her, kissed her on her cheek and said, "Good morning mother, I love you." She sadly looked at him, her eyes puffy from crying, kissed him on his forehead and said, "Good morning son, I love you too, I love all ya'll, go get ready for school." Robbie knew what was wrong with her, but the other children didn't, they went to kiss Grace and saw how sad she was. They all became worried and asked her what was wrong. Grace replied, "Mama is ok, I just have a headache that's all now you all go and get ready for school and I am going to fix you something to eat for breakfast." They all said ok and went to get dressed.

Robbie felt worn out. He was tired of this routine happening again and again. Anthony always did something to hurt Grace or make her mad and she would end up in the same predicament. He wondered if it was normal for love to make a person feel this way and if it was, he never wanted to be in love with anybody. The children finished getting ready for school, ate their breakfast, then Grace told them to get into the car so that she could drop them off. As they walked out they noticed Anthony sitting on the front porch, smoking a cigarette. It seemed as if he had been there for a while. The children each walked by him and he said nothing to them, he just stared at them with contempt. They didn't care, they just got into the car and waited on Grace to come out.

While they waited, Laura said, "What's wrong with him? Why is he looking at us like that?" Robbie said, "Because he probably mad about something but who cares? I know I don't care if he mad or not." Robbie hated Anthony, so he did everything he could to provoke him because he knew that Anthony hated him as well. Robbie stared at Anthony in disgust, never shifting his gaze. He wanted Anthony to see the hate and know that he wasn't afraid of him. Anthony and Robbie glared at each other for at least five minutes. Anthony wished Robbie was dead and the feeling was mutual. They were so engrossed in glaring at each other that neither of them noticed Grace standing in the doorway watching the stare down. She yelled, "Boy get your seat belt on." Robbie jumped from being caught off guard and quickly put his seat belt on. Grace stood there for a moment pondering why a grown ass man was staring at a child the way Anthony just did. As she walked past Anthony, he said something to her, but she ignored him as if he didn't exist. She got into the car, put her seat belt on, sat back and took a deep breath as if she was trying to release all of the stress and to prepared for what the day would bring. She cranked the car up and put her hand on the gear stick, Robbie placed his hand on top of hers and said, "Mother it will be ok, and I promise you it will be ok." She looked at him grinned and said, "I know baby boy, I know." As she put the car in reverse to back out of the driveway, Robbie was the only one to look back to see Anthony still staring angrily.

Robbie was so tired of him hurting Grace, she didn't deserve it. Anthony took advantage of Grace's love for him and every chance that he got, he used it against her to hurt her more. Robbie and Laura were the last ones to be dropped off. He let her get out of the car first because he wanted to say something to their mother. Laura kissed Grace and got out, Grace looked at Robbie and said, "Have a good day son, I want you to learn something ok." Robbie stared at Grace, not blinking at all. He was looking into her eyes and it made him so angry that his beautiful mother, who had a heart of gold, was sitting with so much hurt in her eyes. He couldn't understand why anybody would hurt her. He was always the one to tell her how pretty she was and that he loved her no matter what because that's what she deserved. He was in such a daze that he didn't respond to Grace telling me to have a good day in school, so she said it again, "Son what's a matter? Do you hear me talking to you boy? Are you ok? Why are you looking at me like that?" It was making her a little nervous because she had never seen Robbie looking so serious before. He took her hand and said, "Mama I am sorry for fighting Jake and hurting your feelings by laughing when you hit me, I don't know what it was that made me do that. I don't like Anthony mama and I was mad with you because you let him come back home." She replied, "Son your mama knows more than you think she know, I had you and I can feel when something is wrong. I know that there is something that you are not telling me, and I saw how you two were looking at each other this morning and I am going to figure it out. I am not mad with you so don't get worried but if there is something that you need to tell me you can always talk to your mama. I know you don't like him, and I know you don't like him seeing your mother upset, but let me handle this my way ok? Mama is going to be alright, you don't have to worry about that son." She was in tears and it made Robbie cry as well due to his anger at seeing Grace upset enough to cry.

Robbie had a lot of anger built up inside. He wanted to tell Grace the truth, but he knew that if he did, she would kill Anthony or try to and he would blame himself if the end result was her leaving them to go to jail. Robbie was crying hard and Grace put her arms around him, hugging him tight. She put her hands on his face, to wipe his tears and said, "Son please don't cry, I am going to be ok, everything is going to be ok. Look at me!" Robbie looked at her and she said, "I deal with so much and I know that ya'll see it every day, and this hurts me to see my kids watch me go through all this drama, but I promise you son sooner or later I am going to make the right decision. I am not perfect I have made some bad choices in my life, but I want you to know that I am not going to keep putting my babies through this shit so please stop crying for mama ok." For some reason, although he tried, Robbie couldn't stop crying. When you love someone as much as he loved his mother, it hurt him to see her hurting more than any of the abuse ever had. He just wanted to protect her. She'd become accustomed to being hurt, she followed the same patters again and again. She'd been in relationships with sorry ass man after sorry ass man. Witnessing the pain, she suffered would eventually make it difficult for Robbie to trust anyone. And he hated the idea of romantic love. Robbie felt justified in being anti-social and guarded. He didn't want to talk to anyone, form relationships with anyone, it made him shut down emotionally. In that moment, Robbie hated the world. He was numb to love and was starting to lose his faith in God. He'd prayed every night for God to get his family out of this mess and every time he had hope that his prayers had been answered, Anthony always came back. And every time Anthony came back, Grace would get hurt again and Robbie would be back to being abused. This cycle of pain made Robbie question why God would allow him and his family to be put through all of this. He couldn't understand how an almighty God seemed unable to save them. Why would God let little kids like him get abused in the first place? How could He let anybody harm His kids?

Grace had pulled into a parking space at the school so that Robbie could calm down and stop crying. He finally stopped and looked said to grace, "Thank you for being my mama, I will have a good day and I will learn something. I am going to make you proud one day and I am going to take care of you I promise." She smiled and replied, "You have already made me proud son, I know that you are going to take care of me when you get older and I can't wait. Now get inside before you are late for class." Robbie got out of the car ran to get into the school building. Before he went in, he stopped to see where Grace was, to watch her drive off. To his surprise she was still smiling and watching him as he stood in the doorway. Robbie thought about how much his mother loved him, and he was still worried about her emotional wellbeing. He hoped that nothing bad happened while he was at school and didn't want to come home to police cars in the yard. He said to himself as he walked, "You are not going to worry, everything is going to be ok, mama is going to be fine, focus on school and don't worry about anything else. Make your mama proud!" He walked into class and started his day with a smile and the rest of the day went with no worries.

At the end of the school day, the bell rang, and Robbie started his daily journey to pick up his siblings. He was hoping that Grace would be outside to pick him up, but she wasn't, the worries started to creep back in. As he walked his normal route, he noticed that it was a beautiful day outside, the wind was calm, the sun was out, it was not too hot or too cold. It felt so good that Robbie started singing his one of his favorite songs "Let's Groove" by one of his favorite groups, 'Earth, Wind & Fire'. He had an old soul, a lot of people said that he had been on earth before, so he knew how to groove. Robbie loved music, his mother told him that even when he was a baby any kind of music would make him stop what he was doing and start to dance. Grace would also play this particular song at her parties and Robbie would sit by the door to listen. He didn't know what it was about that song, but he fell in love with it and would continue to sing this song whenever he felt good. Robbie used to love watching the people at parties groove to the music. Robbie was a performer, anytime he sang a song he would do so with exaggerated dance moves as if he was on stage. As he walked he closed his eyes and let his imagination transform him into the lead singer of Earth, Wind & Fire, Maurice White. He could see himself in those nice glowing outfits they wore, and he began to sing, "Let's groove tonight, share the spice of life, baby slice it right we're gonna grove tonight." Robbie was in his own world, he was doing his dance routine, getting deep into his groove and he didn't care who was watching. He was locked in, grooving and having a good time. Cars were driving by him, honking their horns amused to see a little boy dancing down the sidewalk. One lady even yelled out the window, "Get it baby! Go head now! I see you!" He had no cares in the world, this was his moment it was how he was able to escape his real-world stressors. Robbie was having a great time, he was so zoned out that he didn't notice that he was being followed. Suddenly he heard a car and looked back to see Grace's car. She had been watching the whole time and Robbie didn't even notice. Normally he would be embarrassed, sometimes he felt a little shy. But Grace pulled up beside him with the biggest smile on her face, Laura was in the front seat, Tori and Jake were in the back. Grace's smile was all Robbie needed to get him pumped up. He started to dance and continue on with his show, Grace yelled out, "That's my son! He is going to be famous one day!" Robbie was so happy, he didn't expect Grace to pick them up after school due to all the stress she had experienced the previous night. Grace seemed unbothered and in a very good mood. Robbie was still dancing and singing when Grace stopped the car and said, "Come on boy get in the back we've got things to do."

Robbie wondered what in the world they had to do but he didn't care as long as Anthony was not with them. He got in the back seat of the car, hugged Grace from behind, kissed her on her cheek, put his seatbelt on. Grace was always jamming when she drove, she had her music playing and her sunglasses on. Music helped her relax. Robbie had no clue where they were headed but they were soon driving on the highway which was not the way to go home. It made Robbie happy to listen to his mother sing to the music as she drove. There was no Anthony just Grace and her children.

CHAPTER
19

S oon the family was deep into the country and pulled up a long drive way onto a farm. There were a bunch of their family members out there, some of them were riding mopeds and bikes. They were drinking, cooking on the grill, playing football, horseshoes, racing each other on foot, and listening to some good cook out music for the soul. As they pulled up Robbie said, "Mama when are we going to do our homework?" She replied, "Don't worry about that right now, when we get home you can do it but right now I want you to have fun and enjoy yourselves with your cousins." She didn't have to tell him twice, Robbie opened his door and took off straight for the foot race and mopeds. He always felt like he was the fastest kid alive and his family members were all so fast and athletic, but he didn't care. He was the smallest, but he was determined to race with the big boys.

The cousins were all big, country boys who were very competitive. But even though Robbie was small, they didn't take it easy on him, they usually treated him like a big boy. Robbie's favorite cousin, he nick-named 'Super Hero', he looked up to him like he was a big brother. Every time he saw Robbie, Super Hero would get excited and pick him up like he missed him. Super Hero was so fast and strong, that Robbie wanted to be just like him. Robbie had no real father figure to look up to, so every chance he got to see an alpha male, he embraced it. Robbie learned so much about how to handle life when his cousin was around. No matter how much time had passed between their visits, he always mentored Robbie and talked to him about all the things he should know. Robbie watched the foot races and saw that nobody was able to beat Super Hero. He finally built up the courage to ask if he could race with them. Super Hero looked up excitedly and ran over to him, picking him up and spinning him around. He was so happy to see Robbie, he said, "Hey big head you sure you ready to run with the big boys?" Robbie replied, "Yep I been ready so who am I racing first?" There were at least 10 people racing, men and women family members who were all competitive. Their family known for speed, there were athletic stars all throughout their family. Even when the women raced against the men they would hold their own.

Super Hero had them all line up four at a time and the fastest two out of the four would advance to the semifinals and then the finals. Robbie always tried to impress Super Hero, so he wanted to make it to the finals, he knew that there were cousins who were faster than him a long time ago, but they didn't know that he had been practicing. He was ready to surprise them all and show them how much he had improved. This was all love and fun, the family was very close, and Robbie loved to get away from the crazy part of life to have fun at the gatherings.

Robbie was the youngest out of the racers, so their first instinct was to baby him and assume that he wasn't fast enough to race them. So, they put him in a group where nobody was faster than him. Robbie was smiling on the inside because he knew that he was going to win but he had to be strategic about it, he wondered to himself if he should go all out or do just enough to win. He wanted to surprise everyone, so he decided to do just enough to barely win the semifinals then he would give his all in the final race. Robbie ran just fast enough to get second place in the semifinals because he knew it was enough to advance him to the final race. Robbie saw Grace and his siblings watching along with all of the other family members, so he knew he had to make it look good. Grace knew that Robbie was fast, but she didn't know that he had improved so much in the last few months. Super Hero put his hands up in the air to give them the signal, Robbie got in his starting stance just like the track stars that he saw on television and everybody was looked at him with shock and surprise. Super Hero looked around and said, "Runners take your mark." Robbie was ready, zoned out as if he was running for the Olympics, he heard, "Get set!" he raised up and it was show time when he heard, "Go!"

Robbie took off like a bat out of hell, his eyes were closed, and he could hear the sound of the wind going as he sprinted forward. Robbie was way ahead of the pack, so he deliberately slowed down so he could get second place. The family were cheering Robbie on, they had no idea he was fast enough to get second place! Grace was grinning from ear to ear, so proud of him. Super Hero ran up to Robbie with an amazed look on his face asking, "Man what have you been doing? You are fast boy! You could have won easy, I have to teach you how I do it, so you can hang with the big boys!" All Robbie did was smile because he knew he was more than ready for the big boys. He was about to really show off his skills.

Robbie went up to Grace and she gave him big hug and kissed him on his forehead. She was so proud, she said, "Son you are just like your mama boy! I didn't know you were that fast at all! You made it to the big boys' level now you have to show them how it's done!" Robbie replied, "Yes mama I will, I been practicing so they will see." He felt amazing, he loved making Grace happy and seeing that beautiful smile. She had made the right decision for herself and the children by going out to the country to spend time with their extended family. This love and positivity was exactly what they needed after having such chaos happening at home.

The family was still in shock by how Robbie, the youngest of the participants, was able to run so fast. Robbie was in his zone, he let his imagination take over and was treating it like a real track meet. After the initial race there were four more races that would occur before the final races. All of the fastest cousin in the family advanced through the rounds including one female cousin. Robbie stood and watched, making mental notes of how they ran, their breathing, and their form. He planned to modify his technique to incorporate what he thought were the best techniques to improve his racing. Super Hero was up next to run in the last of the semifinals. He would usually ask one of his older cousins to call the race, but he decided to have Robbie call it. He said, "Robbie, I want you to call it, so you can see how I run and that way when you run in the finals you will do a lot better and hopefully come in fourth." This further motivated Robbie because Super Hero was already underestimating Robbie's abilities. But that was a part of his plan, to be underestimated and shock them all. Robbie smiled at him and said, "Ok I will watch you." He walked to the finish line so that he could call the race. He was amused because Super Hero seemed to think Robbie would do good to come in fourth place. Robbie loved being the underdog, it was a quality he had in common with his mother, they loved to prove people wrong.

Grace was really good at nearly everything that she did. She had always been extremely athletic, she was fast, could play basketball, football, softball and more. Robbie thought back to one time when he saw his mother race his older, male cousins. She raced them barefoot because she didn't have sneakers on that day and she beat them in the race. Robbie put extra pressure on himself to live up to Grace's reputation. There was no way that he would allow himself to come in fourth place. He'd run his hardest and fastest with the expectation of getting first or second place. Robbie made his way to the finish line and yelled out, "Are ya'll ready?" They all said yes, he glanced over at Super Hero he who was smiling and confident. Super Hero knew that he was going to win easily, and it almost seemed as if he didn't take the race seriously. Everybody got into position and Super Hero was the last to take his mark. Robbie watched how he was comfortable and relaxed with no worries in the world. Robbie put his hands up and said, "Runners take your mark, get set, go!" They all bolted straight ahead for the finish line, Super Hero was running steadily, just enough to let the racers think they had a chance at winning. His stride was phenomenal, but he was running out of time, they had at least, twenty meters to go and he was still behind. The family members were all hooting and hollering, cheering everyone on, thinking that this time someone else might beat Super Hero. Robbie was starting to get worried because Super Hero was still behind at the ten-meter mark, if he had lost this would be the upset of the entire family. But Super Hero actually had a similar strategy to Robbie's, he was purposely running slower to allow the other racers to think they'd win. All of a sudden, he sped up and ended up beating everyone by five meters. Robbie was amazed, as Super Hero just grinned and strutted around looking at everyone as if he was the king. One of the cousins, Larry, was a sore loser, he got mad and started crying falling out all over the place throwing a fit because he expected to be a finalist. Larry was a spoiled brat, looked at Super Hero and said, "That's not fair you always win every time I don't like you!" Super Hero replied back, "Boy shut up and learn how to run faster, stop whining and go somewhere and sit down." That's exactly what Larry did after being told to sit down. Super Hero walked up to Robbie, with a smile plastered across his face. He said, "See how I run, I want you to do the same thing, so you can be faster than me one day!" Robbie loved Super Hero, he idolized him, but he had his own plans. Robbie planned on beating his idol in the next race.

Robbie always imagined that he had super hero powers because he was so athletic and good at any sport he tried. He kept it a secret from most people because he was dealing with the abuse from Anthony. And the drama that came along with that left him very little time to participate in organized sports. But in school, Robbie always won first place at his school's field day events, nobody was faster than him, but he never took his ribbons home because he thought that Anthony would take them and destroy them. So, Robbie kept any awards and ribbons he'd earned in his cubby at school.

There was a lot that the family didn't know, the children never went anywhere or did anything because Grace was always working. Most of them could tell that the children didn't get out much, but they understood the situation. Robbie looked at Super Hero, smiled and tapped him on his shoulders saying, "Ok I will do that because I do want to be just like you one day!" He replied, "You will, you got the potential, you just have to keep practicing. We will do the final race in ten minutes so go stretch because you are running with the best of the best." Robbie agreed and walked over to Grace where she was sitting. She was talking with one of the nosiest cousins in the family, Chrissy, always in everybody's business. Robbie went and gave Grace a hug, then stood beside her. Chrissy said to Robbie, "You love your mama, don't you?" Robbie replied, "Yes ma'am." She was chewing gum and was smacking so loud and it was nerve wrecking. Chrissy put her hands out, gesturing for Robbie to hug her and said, "Come here big head and give me a hug stop being a mama's boy she is not going anywhere." A flash of annoyance crossed his face, but he went over to give her a hug. Robbie felt as though it was unnecessary for her to say what she did about him being a mama's boy because that was none of her concern. But out of respect for his elders, he quickly obliged the request for a hug, then walked back to where Grace was standing. Chrissy loved to pry into people's business and Robbie knew what was coming next as she smacked on her gum, looking them up and down. She looked at Grace and asked how she and Anthony were doing. Robbie thought to himself, now is not the time, and Grace replied, "We are doing ok." She gave Grace an odd look as if she knew she was lying, and she said, "That's good but why don't he ever come with ya'll? I heard what happened at the family reunion, we are not going to bite him he is more than welcome." Grace was getting irritated and Chrissy could tell but she didn't back down. Grace replied, "He stay busy, but he will be at the next thing that we do. The family reunion is what it is, people have issues in relationships, they overcome them, and we did." Chrissy was still chewing her bubble gum, being messy when another cousin, Doris walked up. Chrissy looked at Doris and told her, "Grace says Anthony stay busy, and that's why he didn't come but I told her to tell him that we are ok with him." Doris looked at Chrissy and said, "Oh ok girl, yeah we love everybody he is family too." Grace couldn't stand nosey ass people and from the look on her face she was getting fed up so of Chrissy decided to direct her questions towards Robbie. She asked him, "You like him?" Robbie responded, "Like who?" She replied, "Anthony. He seems to make your mama happy." Before Robbie could respond, Grace interrupted and said, "He love him, do your kids like your new boyfriend?" Chrissy replied, "I am sorry if I said anything wrong, I was just making conversation, and yes my babies love my sweet heart."

Grace got up from the chair that she was sitting in, looked at Robbie and said, "Come on son, y'all are about to race." Robbie said ok, then looked back at Doris and Chrissy to say good bye. Then they headed over to the field that was being used for the races. As they walked to the field, Robbie noticed that Grace was upset about Chrissy's meddling. She was walking really fast and mumbling mean things like, "Damn bitch need to mind her own business, she is not even our real cousin with her ugly ass self." Robbie took Grace's hand and said, "Mama Miss Chrissy was getting on my nerves." She replied, "Yeah she was getting on mine too, she better be glad that I didn't whoop her ass, with her stinking breath." Robbie laughed, Grace was so funny when she was upset, and he got a kick out of hearing her cuss people out.

Robbie was so much like Grace, personality wise, in moments like these, he could tell that he'd inherited his mean streak from her. As they got closer to the field they could see the big boys gearing up for the race, they were stretching, running quick sprints, and getting ready for the show down. Grace looked at Robbie and said, "I want you to do the damn thing son! I know you are going to beat all of them even Superman. I know my child, you got your mama blood in you, they don't know what's about to happen, but I do." Hearing Grace say that was an awesome feeling for Robbie, she really believed in him and had faith in his talents even though he was so young. The cousins were all at least six years older than Robbie so beating them would be extraordinary. Robbie knew that his super hero speed would kick in and he would beat everyone. His only concern was how his favorite cousin would respond to being beaten in a race by him. Super Hero had always been used to winning every race and being the fastest in the family. Robbie replied back to Grace, "Thank you mama, I am going to beat them all just for you! But what if Super Hero gets mad at me for beating him? Then he won't like me anymore." Grace took his face, put her hands on his cheeks and said, "Look at me son, don't hide what talent God gave you, run your race to the best of your ability, don't worry about nobody liking you or not. Super Hero is your cousin he will love you regardless, you know that. So if you beat him…so be it! You show these boys that you are a big boy and you make your mama proud." Something about Grace was that she always knew how to make Robbie feel like he was the greatest kid to ever walk the earth. She was his biggest cheerleader. Robbie replied, "Ok mama it's on, and time to represent." He gave Grace a high five and walked over to get ready for the race.

Everyone looked over at Robbie and asked if he was ready, he smiled and nodded his head as he began to stretch. Then, before the race started he decided to be a good sport and encourage everyone by walking up to each of them to shake their hands, telling them he'd see them at the finish line. They didn't take him seriously and laughed to themselves, but Robbie expected that response from them. He was used to being underestimated and he'd learned to make it work for him in many ways. Super Hero walked up and looked at Robbie with that famous grin and said, "Run as hard as you can and try to get fourth place." He replied, "Ok but I want you to run beside me and I don't want you to take it easy on me as a matter of fact I want everybody to run as hard as they can." He seemed shocked by what Robbie requested but he said, "Ok little cousin, I will tell everybody to run hard, but I want you to know that when we dust you I don't want you to get mad or cry I want you to come back next year and try again ok." Robbie was amused at the idea that Super Hero's expectations of him were so low. Now he was ready to do his thing.

Everybody headed to the starting line, the whole family was watching, this was a big deal, they all loved to compete and have a good time. Robbie could hear Grace screaming, "Come on son! Show these big boys what you got!" He made his way to the middle of the racers, beside Super Hero and everybody was looked over at him like he'd done something wrong. Robbie was not willing to let that distract or discourage him though. He was focused. One of the female cousins who was calling the race instructed them all to get into position. Suddenly Robbie took his mind to a whole new mode, one of anger and violence. He figured that in order to give it everything he had, he needed to run as if he was mad about something. There was nothing that could have made him madder than thinking about Anthony. He imagined that the finish line was tied up with a gun pointing to Anthony's head and if he made it first, the gun would go off and blow Anthony's head to pieces. Robbie looked at Super Hero and he seemed to be nervous from the look in his eyes, he knew that something was about to go down, so it made him get focused as well. The racers were down and waiting for the signal, she yelled, "Runners take your mark, get set, go!" Robbie closed his eyes and took off like a rocket, he could hear everybody screaming for him and Super Hero, he felt their hands touch his right side which meant that they were running neck and neck, but Robbie didn't open his eyes because he was zoned out. He knew that he had to win so he let his thoughts wander to an even angrier dark place. Robbie thought about how Anthony beat him over and over, how he'd choked him until he almost died, how he put his face in the mud and stepped on his head, how he tortured him when Grace went to work, and how he hurt Grace. All of this built up inside of him took Robbie to a level, beyond super hero speed, he started to cry from all of the emotions built up inside. In his mind, he felt that if he made it to the finish line first, that imaginary gun would go off, Anthony would die, and they would live happily ever after. Every stride that Robbie took, he felt the pain, the hurt, the burn, the feeling of being near death so it pushed him even harder as he ran.

The tears ran down his eyes, and he no longer felt Super Hero's hand touch his, he heard nothing but Anthony's voice yelling as he beat him. By the time Robbie opened his eyes, he had passed the finish line. He looked back and they were all still running and just crossing the finish line. The sheer emotion he felt caused him to drop to his knees and cry. He hated Anthony with everything in him and crossing that finish line had killed Anthony in his imagination. And he wished it was true in real life. All of the pain and anger that Robbie carried on a daily basis propelled him across the finish line and there was some relief in releasing some of the emotions by running this race. But once Robbie had started crying, he couldn't stop. The family all ran up to him thinking that something was wrong with him or maybe he'd hurt himself during the race. Grace picked him up, asking if he was ok. She said "What's wrong son you won. You beat everybody, why are you crying like this?" Robbie replied, "I can't tell you right now mama I just can't." Everybody was stared with a mixture of confusion and shock, but they were all glad that he was ok. The race had taken a lot out of him mentally. He hadn't understood the extent of the way he was being impacted by his home life. The things that Anthony did to him were permanently etched into his brain like a tattoo. Every time that Robbie tried to get away from those thoughts, he couldn't.

The crowed was going crazy with excitement and amazement that Robbie had beaten everyone by fifteen meters. They kept telling Grace that she needed to put him in track and field because they had never seen a kid so young run so fast. Grace was so proud, but she was worried because of the emotional breakdown Robbie had at the end of the race. After Robbie calmed down he started looking for Super Hero, he'd lost sight of him. He began asking around to see where he went and was told that he'd gone in the house. Robbie asked Grace if he could go inside to find him and she nodded yes. He headed inside and found Super Hero laying across the bed in his room with a pillow over his face. Robbie's first thought was that Super Hero was mad that he'd beaten him in the race and the realization that he was no longer the fastest in the family. Robbie's heart sank for a moment as he tried to prepare for how Super Hero would treat him. He expected him to be mean to him, but he remembered what Grace had told him. He decided that if he needed to, he would just give Super Hero some space until he calmed down. Robbie stood in the doorway for a few minutes and Super Hero knew he was there but still hadn't said anything to acknowledge him. As Robbie turned to walk away he heard Super Hero say, "Why are you just standing there and not talking?" Robbie responded, "I didn't know if you were mad at me or not and I didn't want to stop being your favorite cousin." He took the pillow off his head, sat up on the bed looked at Robbie and said, "How did you get so fast that quick? It was like something lifted you off the ground and you flew to the finish line." Robbie replied, "I just practice a lot when nobody is watching me." Super Hero crossed his arms and said, "So you knew the whole time that you could beat me?" Robbie looked away shyly and replied, "Kind of, I mean, I knew that I was going to beat everyone else but not you. I want to be just like you, I look up to you, and I didn't mean to beat you because I didn't want you to be mad with me." He motioned for Robbie to come and sit beside him and replied, "Don't ever apologize for beating somebody fair and square. I admit I was upset because I'm not used to losing but I was upset with myself, not you. You have a natural talent that can take you all over the world cousin. I have never seen a kid your age run that fast. You just made me want to work harder that's all." Robbie smiled, put his hand on Super Hero's shoulder and said, "Thank you cousin. You are fast too. You will be the first to win all your races and then when I get bigger I can follow behind you." He replied, "No cousin, you have to start now and then we both can take over the game! That would be so dope me and my little cousin who's already faster than me!" Robbie was so glad to know that Super Hero wasn't mad with him. He didn't know but he was the only male figure that Robbie had in his life to emulate. They continued talking as they headed back outside to eat some of the cook out food that was ready. As they walked out he asked Robbie what he had been thinking about while he was running the race. He said, "At one point during the race you just took off and why were you crying?" Robbie wasn't prepared to discuss these things with him. He knew that if he'd told him the truth about what Anthony had been doing to him, it would have gotten back to the other family members and then there would have been a big mess. He hung his head in shame and said, "I wasn't thinking about nothing at all." Super Hero knew he was lying so he said, "Cousin, you were crying like there was no tomorrow, you were running like you had a purpose, like your life depended on it and I felt it too. You can always talk to me about anything and I promise you I won't tell anybody." Robbie replied, "I know, and I promise you that I will tell you when I know I can." He really did want to tell him, but he couldn't risk the chance of Super Hero running and telling the other family members. They continued to talk as they headed outside to join the rest of the family and Robbie felt special to have earned the respect of his role model. It gave him a boost of confidence that he never had before. Everyone was dancing and having a good time when the two of them walked up. Then they turned when they saw them and said, "There goes the two fastest men in our family!" Robbie and Super Hero looked at each other grinning and started to party with everyone else.

It was getting late, time to head back home. Grace loaded everyone into the car, all of the kids were asleep except for Robbie. Everyone said their goodbyes, Grace turned on her music and they drove off. Robbie's mood went from being happy to depressed, in a matter of minutes. He hated knowing that Anthony would be home when they got back and just the thought of seeing him made Robbie's stomach do flip flops. As they drove, Grace turned down the radio and said, "You know that I am proud of you right?" Robbie replied, "Yes ma'am." She turned the light on inside of the car and she said, "What's wrong son, why are you acting sad?" He replied, "Nothing mama I will be ok." She said, "Don't you nothing me boy, what's wrong with you?" Robbie said, "I just don't want to go back home." Grace stopped the car and they sat parked on the side of the road for a moment and she stared straight ahead as if she was in deep thought. Then she looked at Robbie and said, "I need you to be my big boy ok? You proved to me today that you are a big boy, so I need you to man up son. I know you don't want to go back there and right now I don't blame you but please just let me work through this, so I can put ya'll in a better place. Will you do that for me?" Robbie replied, "Yes ma'am." She turned the music back up and went back to driving. Robbie had a feeling that must have mirrored what it felt like to be headed to prison for the rest of his life. But he tried to put on a brave face for Grace.

CHAPTER
20

obbie had never felt more stuck in this life he was living. He would rather have been homeless than to live in the same house as Anthony. The thought of him made his skin crawl. As they got closer to home Robbie could feel Grace staring at him, then she turned to look at his siblings. Robbie knew it was bothering her that he felt the way he did. He knew she was beating herself up for putting them through the drama of her relationship. When they pulled up to the house, all of the lights were off, and Robbie was hoping that Anthony was not inside. Grace told him to wake his siblings up and he did as she asked. They unloaded the car and headed inside. Robbie could hear Anthony snoring like a hibernating bear. He was there in Grace's room knocked out asleep. Robbie wished he could get a knife and stab him.

Grace told the children not to worry about their homework and to put their night clothes on and get in the bed. They were all in bed in a matter of minutes, tired from the busy day. Robbie was asleep as soon as his head hit the pillow. There was no school for the children the following day. Robbie assumed that they would have to stay home while Grace worked. He got up and walked past his sisters' room and they were gone which was odd because he thought that Grace would have told them that they would be going somewhere. Anthony was still snoring, so it dawned on him that he and Jake had been left there alone with him. Robbie started to panic because he knew that once Anthony woke up and realized that they were alone with him he would finally get his pay back. Robbie was so upset with his mother, he couldn't understand why she would leave them there alone with him. Even though she didn't know about the abuse, she knew that Robbie didn't like him. He had to do something quick. Robbie ran back into the room to wake up Jake. He slept like a rock, so Robbie had to really shake him to get him up and going. As Robbie shook him he moaned and groaned like he didn't want to be woken up. Robbie whispered, "Wake up, get up and put some clothes on but be quiet." Jake was not a morning person, so he screamed, "Leave me alone I am still sleepy!" This was the last thing that Robbie wanted him to do. He was so mad that he threw Jake off of the bed. He jumped up angrily and yelled, "I am going to tell mama what you did!" He went to open the door and Anthony was standing right there, glaring at the two of them. He pushed Jake down on the ground slammed the door into the wall saying, "What the fuck are ya'll little motherfuckers doing in here!" Jake was so startled that he started crying and shaking, which made Anthony even madder. Neither child responded so he screamed, "Do ya'll fucking hear me? Somebody better start talking or else I am going to beat the both of ya'll asses for waking me up out of my sleep!"

Robbie already knew what time it was, he was about to go through hell until Grace got back home. Jake said quietly, "He woke me up and I didn't want to wake up." Anthony interrupted him and angrily shouted, "Boy speak the fuck up before I go upside your head! Stop talking like a little bitch and tell me what happened!" Jake was shaking, he couldn't talk, and he was stuttering and crying so bad that he couldn't tell on Robbie. Anthony knock on the door with his fist pointed to Jake and said, "Boy bring your ass here now!" Robbie was not about to let him hurt his brother, he'd promised to protect him no matter what. Even though he was trying to tell on him, Robbie would protect him from Anthony. Suddenly Anthony drew his hand back to hit Jake and Robbie jumped in front of him to shield him, screaming "NO! NO! I did it, I tried to wake him up so that we could eat breakfast and he didn't want to get up, so I pushed him off of the bed! It wasn't his fault it was mine!" Before he could blink Robbie saw stars and was on the floor, Anthony had hit him, and it knocked him down. All he could hear was Jake crying and screaming, "Leave my brother alone, please get up!" Anthony yelled at Jake, "Get your fucking ass in that kitchen and sit down!" He put his hand around Robbie's neck and yelled, "Get your fucking ass up nigga! You want to be a man huh! It's been a long fucking time since we played!"

Robbie was in a daze. Anthony had punched him in the forehead and he couldn't focus. He felt Anthony's hand getting tighter and tighter around his neck until he threw him onto the bed and started yelling at him and pacing frantically. Anthony screamed at him, "You are the devil's child! God told me to punish you! You are a fucking demon! You have to learn nigga! I prayed for you boy do you hear me? I prayed for you and God gave me this day to teach you a lesson!" Robbie was shocked by what he was hearing. He'd called him the devil's child, he wondered what the hell was going on in Anthony's brain. What had he done to make him think that Robbie needed to be punished? Anthony was the demon, Robbie thought. He was completely insane. He just knew that Anthony would eventually kill him. None of what he was saying made any sense so instinctively, Robbie sat there and stared at the ground as Anthony stared at him, breathing heavily. He could feel Anthony's gaze as if it was burning a hole through his flesh. Robbie was determined not to look up at him because he knew that if he did, Anthony would have gone even further into a rage. Robbie was trying his best to avoid being hit again. Eventually Anthony's breathing slowed, and Robbie thought he had calmed down but he yelled "Sit up and look at me like you were looking at me yesterday little nigga! Look me in his eyes like a man and show me how big and bad you are! Mama is nowhere around to save you nigga! Look at me!" Robbie slowly looked up at him and stared into his eyes. Anthony moved closer to him, so close that he was in Robbie's face with their noses nearly touching. Anthony was breathing hard and fast, his breath was making Robbie nauseous, as it stunk like cigarettes and alcohol. He pressed his forehead onto Robbie's and said, "Yeah nigga this what you want huh? You want me to be your little bitch, don't you? You want to be the king, don't you?" He balled his hand into a fist and said "Open your mouth nigga! Open it wide too." Robbie glared at him defiantly and Anthony slapped him hard, across the face, three times and screamed, "Open your fucking mouth nigga!" Tears started streamed down Robbie's face, he was so angry, but he did what Anthony told him to do. When Robbie opened his mouth, Anthony tried to put his entire fist into his mouth and instinctively Robbie tried to pull away. Anthony grabbed the back of Robbie's head with his other hand trying to force his fist into Robbie's mouth and started yelling out as if he was getting physical pleasure from Robbie's pain. Anthony's knuckles pressed into Robbie's teeth causing his skin to break and bleed. When Anthony saw the blood, he slapped Robbie again with all of his strength and yelled, "You little bitch, you bit me and made me bleed!" He slapped him again and said "Suck my blood boy! Suck it all off!" Then he put his bloody knuckle in Robbie's mouth. In fear of what might happen next, Robbie sucked the blood off of his knuckle. He was so horrified at what was happening he became nauseous with the thought of contracting Anthony's germs and whatever else that he started to wretch. Anthony pushed Robbie's head back and said, "Good boy now kiss it and make it all better like my mama used to do!" Robbie was reaching his breaking point, he couldn't force himself to kiss Anthony's knuckle after having sucked his blood. He made up his mind that Anthony would just have to kill him.

Anthony saw that Robbie wouldn't kiss his knuckle, so he sat back, smiled and said, "Oh ok you and I got all day to play, your mama stupid ass actually thought that I wanted to spend some quality time with her two pussy ass boys! She thought that I wanted to do better and bond with ya'll." He laughed out loud and said, "Fuck ya'll little niggas, I can't stand ya'll soft asses! I just told her that so that I could get my last little moments of play time with you! I missed you little nigga! This is how we bond! You think I'm stupid, I know your mama don't want me no more, so until I am gone I am going to fuck with you every day!"

Robbie, feeling defeated wondered to himself what his mother had been thinking. She had fallen into Anthony's trap again! How could she believe this crazy man! She took the girls with her so that he could spend time with the boys so that meant that she was trying to work things out with him. Robbie was so upset with her. He felt betrayed and like Grace had lied to him. The boys would be stuck with Anthony all day long. Suddenly Anthony told Robbie to go in the kitchen to fix him and Jake some cereal. As he walked by, he pushed Robbie into the door and told him to hurry up. Robbie hated his guts! He didn't understand what he had ever done to be treated this way. Robbie slowly walked to the kitchen, sad and depressed, hating life and thinking he'd rather kill himself than be tortured by Anthony. But as usual, when Robbie had those thoughts he talked himself out of it. Even though killing himself would mean that he wouldn't have to endure the abuse anymore, he knew that would hurt his family. He also didn't want to feel like he'd let Anthony defeat him.

When he made it to the kitchen, Robbie saw Jake sitting at the table with a frightened and sad look on his face. Robbie just whispered to him, "It's ok don't be sad ok." He knew then that had to be strong or Jake would end up going through everything that had happened to him. Robbie began making the bowls of cereal for the two of them when he noticed how quiet it was and figured that Anthony must be listening to what he was saying to Jake. As Robbie made the bowls of cereal and poured milk into his own bowl after having filled Jake's, he realized that they'd run out of milk. There wasn't enough to pour into his own bowl, but he was ok as he wasn't very hungry anyway. He passed the bowl with the adequate amount of milk in it to Jake, but Jake slid it back to him telling him to eat it. Robbie was getting angry with Jake thinking he must not have realized what Anthony had just done to him and he did not want to be in another situation which would give him a reason to come back out thinking they were arguing. Robbie was already exhausted and sore from his first beating of the day and didn't know that he'd be able to take having another beating so soon. He slid the bowl back to Jake and said, "Please eat this before we get in trouble again." By the time Robbie finished his sentence Anthony walked in the kitchen, making his heart drop. He stood behind Jake putting his hand on his shoulders and Robbie jumped up. Anthony snapped his fingers pointed at him and yelled, "Sit your ass down now nigga! You just don't learn, do you? I told you that you are the devil's child! Who wants to keep get their ass beat but you?" Jake started crying again, and Anthony pulled his chair back, turning it to face him and said to Jake, "What the fuck is wrong with your soft ass? I haven't even touched you so why in the hell are you crying?" Anthony looked at the cereal and milk then looked at Robbie and said, "Where the rest of the milk?" Robbie said, "It's gone that's all that we had left." He replied, "So you are going to waste his damn cereal and not eat anything because you don't have any milk?" Robbie shook his head and said, "No I was going to eat it, I was just trying to give it to him first and then I was going to ask for some money so that I could walk to the store and buy some milk." Anthony burst out laughing and said, "So you were going to ask me could I give you some money to the store and get some milk?" Robbie replied, "Yes sir." He took the bowl that had less milk, walked to the other side of the kitchen, looked out the window and said, as he was still laughing, "Boy you are about the stupidest little nigga I have ever seen! You were going to ask me, the nigga that can't stand your little punk ass to give you my money so that you can spend it on something you need?" Robbie replied, "Yes sir." Anthony said, "So you really want some milk? I am going to make you some of my homemade special milk that is going to get you really big and strong and taste so good!" Robbie did not like the sound of that. He knew how much Anthony hated him and he had never heard of a man making milk without a cow.

He told his Jake to take the cereal to his room and told Robbie to go in there and sit with Jake while he made some milk. Robbie followed Jake into their bedroom and he could feel Anthony watching as they walked away. When they made it to the room, Jake whispered "How is he going to make some milk?" Robbie replied, "I don't know but I am about to find out, you just sit here and eat your cereal, I will be right back." Robbie got up and quietly walked to the corner of the door so that he could peep around the corner into the kitchen and what Anthony was doing to "make milk". Anthony was standing by the refrigerator with his back turned so that if anyone walked in, they wouldn't be able to see exactly what he was doing. His head was down, and he had his shorts pulled down almost to his knees. Robbie thought to himself, "What in the hell is he doing?" He heard what sounded like water running but it wasn't coming from a sink. Suddenly the sound stopped, and Robbie saw him jerk his hand back and forth. As Anthony turned Robbie saw his bowl of cereal in one of his hands as he pulled up his shorts with the other hand. Anthony had urinated in his bowl of cereal!

Robbie looked on in horror thinking that there was no way that he was going to eat that cereal. Anthony grabbed the spoon from the table, stirred the cereal and urine mixture then went to the sink ad added some water to it. Then he started walking towards the boys' room. Robbie ran back over to the bed as if he had just been sitting there waiting. He was in utter disbelief that Anthony was about to give him a bowl of cereal that he'd just pissed in. Anthony walked into the room, handed Robbie the bowl and said, "Here you go boy, I made you some real good milk too and I want you to eat all of it." Robbie took the bowl with a disgusted look on his face and said "Yes Sir" as he sat the bowl in his lap, hoping Anthony would leave. But he stood right there watching and waiting for him to eat it.

Robbie could smell the urine in the bowl and the milk didn't look like it was supposed to look. Anthony walked up in front of him and said, "What are you waiting on boy eat that cereal." Robbie responded that his stomach was hurting. He did not want to put Anthony's urine in his mouth. Anthony turned his head to the side and said, "Boy eat that dam cereal and eat it now." Robbie couldn't do it, he knew what was coming next and he was prepared for it, so he just figured the hell with it and said, "You peed in my cereal, I saw you and I don't want it!" He snatched the bowl away from him, put his foot on Robbie's chest and pressed him up against the wall with it saying "What the fuck do you mean you saw me? So, you spying on me now nigga? Open your mouth now!" Robbie yelled, "No! I am not going to do it!" He took his foot off of Robbie's chest, grabbed his face around his jaw area, took a spoon full of cereal and started to force it down into Robbie's mouth. Robbie tried his best not to let it happen, he could smell the urine all over him and the spoon, but Anthony gripped his jaws so hard that all he could do was open his mouth. He forced Robbie to eat three spoons of his urinated cereal and the whole time Anthony was smiling and laughing like it was funny.

Jake had run out of the room and hid so that he couldn't see what had happened. After Anthony was finished he took the rest of the bowl and dumped it all over Robbie, told him to clean it up and then he walked out of the room. Robbie felt so violated and devastated all he could do was cry. He'd just eaten Anthony's urine and was sitting in a puddle of it. He was in shock and couldn't move at first. Once he was able to calm down he slowly started to clean up the cereal. Robbie could hear Anthony in the bathroom singing as he bathed. Jake had come back into the room, got on the bed and put the pillow over his head. He couldn't look at Robbie because it hurt him that he couldn't help him.

Anthony knew that Robbie wouldn't say anything to Grace because he felt like he him on lock. He knew Robbie was terrified of him, so he had every intention of continuing to abuse him as often as he could. Grace wouldn't be home for several more hours and Robbie didn't know how much more he would be able to take. He knew he'd have no choice but to put up with the abuse until Anthony was tired of messing with him or until she made it home. Robbie was shaking, and his heart was racing every time he thought he heard Anthony make a move because he thought he was coming to get him. Everything was cleaned up, Robbie went in the bathroom and washed up at the sink, feeling more and more defeated when he glanced at his reflection in the mirror. He felt like giving up. Grace had always told him to be proud of what God created when he saw himself in the mirror. She told them that he was a strong, handsome, loving son that she brought into this world and that he needed to be proud because he was powerful and a young king. But as he looked at himself in the mirror all he felt was ashamed. He had drunk Anthony's urine, and he wasn't proud of what God had created in him. Robbie felt that if God created him to be abused He shouldn't have created him at all.

He felt like he was losing his mind. He took a deep breath and opened his eyes, looked at his reflection and said, "He can't hurt you, you are strong, you have to be around to take care of your family, stop hating yourself it's not your fault, you have to find a way to win, make your mind strong!" Robbie took another deep breath and smiled. He had calmed down, gotten his mind prepared and now he was ready for war. He'd seen movies like this where the enemy would torture the hero and do all that he could to break him, but the hero would stay strong. He was strategic, he let the enemy think he had broken him until the time was right and then the hero used all of his strength to overcome and defeat them all. Robbie said to himself, "Be ready no matter what, stay ready, you got this let's go!" He wiped the tears from his eyes and went back into the room with his brother. It was quiet, and Jake had been so exhausted from the stress that he had fallen asleep. Robbie didn't hear Anthony, so he decided to lay down and use the quiet time that he had at the moment to relax until the next storm came.

CHAPTER
21

Robbie had a picture of the Incredible Hulk under his bed. He had always wanted to be like him because he was a regular guy until somebody made him mad. Then he would transform into a big muscular creature and kick some ass when it was time. Robbie knew that one day he would be like the Incredible Hulk. He would have big muscles, be strong and kick ass just like him, that was something he let himself day dream about. He pulled out the picture and stared at it for a while, his thoughts were all over the place and he was trying not to panic about what would happen next while his mother was gone. Robbie began talking to the picture as if the Hulk was there with him. He asked, "How can I be like you now? What is your secret? What do I have to do to get muscles like you and kick Anthony's ass?" Robbie flexed his muscles as hard as he could and began hitting himself in an imitation of the Hulk to see if that would help him transform. To his disappointment, it didn't work. He was strong for his age but that wasn't going to be enough to protect himself from Anthony. In that moment, Robbie made a promise to himself that he would work towards being so big and strong that nobody would mess with him. He stared at the picture some more and began to pace back and forth to channel his thoughts into becoming a beast.

Suddenly, Robbie heard footsteps and quickly stopped pacing to sit on the bed. Anthony came to the door, looked in on the boys and walked away, heading towards the back door. He went outside, lit a cigarette and stood there plotting. Robbie could see him from their bedroom window and reasoned that he was out there thinking of more ways to hurt and torment him. As Robbie watched, Anthony began talking to himself and answering back like he was having a conversation with himself. He would speak and then walk to the other side of the porch and respond back and forth as if he was two different people. Robbie couldn't hear the words that he Anthony was saying but he looked like he was shouting and arguing with himself. Anthony even hit himself in the chest and then picked up a brick and threw it to the other side of the porch as if he meant to hit his other, imaginary self.

Robbie was alarmed by this display, he had never seen anyone do that before. He thought to himself that if Grace had seen Anthony acting this way she would never have involved herself with him. Anthony was clearly mentally disturbed. Robbie was convinced that Anthony was the kind of person who needed to be locked away from the public. In thinking about some of the things Anthony had said to him, calling him the devil's child and talking about how God told him to punish him, he wondered if that was what Anthony's porch "argument" was about. Maybe Anthony believed he was arguing with God, or maybe it was the demons in his mind that had him so upset. Soon, Anthony finished his cigarette and came back inside the house. Robbie quickly sat back down on the bed to try and pretend that he wasn't doing anything. Anthony slowly walked up to the doorway looked in and said, "I know you were watching me, and you are going to get enough of spying on me!" Robbie continued to sit on the bed, deciding not to respond verbally. He knew that anything could set Anthony off and he'd learned over time that any response to his statements would send him into a rage. He stood and stared at Robbie for about five minutes and Robbie still didn't say a word. Robbie knew that he was trying to scare him, so he stopped looking at him and shifted his gaze towards the ground. Anthony said "Hmmm mmm, yeah nigga, that's right, you better know what to do." Repeating this again and again as he walked away. Robbie took a deep breath, stood up, then began to quietly taunt Anthony as if he was still standing there. He was still in the Hulk mindset and began to growl like he was the little Hulk. Robbie decided that it was only a matter of time before he discovered his strength.

Even though he was sore from that morning's beating, Robbie got down on the floor and started to do pushups. It was painful, but he was determined to take that pain and turn it into happiness. Every time Robbie felt that aches in his body from being punched, kicked and slapped he smiled. He knew that despite what Anthony had done, he was overcoming his attempts to make him feel weak and like he was nothing. This mindset, all began with focusing on that picture of one of his favorite superheroes. Robbie had found something inside himself that he never knew he had. Jake woke up, saw Robbie doing pushups and said, "What are you doing and why are you making that noise and smiling?" Robbie replied, "I am turning into the little Incredible Hulk so that I can be strong and beat Anthony up." Jake got down off his bed and said, "You can't be like him, his muscles are too big, and you can't beat Mr. Anthony up because he too big too!" Robbie replied, "Yes I can, and I will show you, you want to get strong too?" Jake said, "Yes." Then he got down and started copying what Robbie had been doing. He was growling and doing little baby pushups. Both boys continued doing pushups until Jake got tired. But Robbie kept going to show his little brother how strong he was. He wanted Jake to believe what he was saying so that if he ever had to go through what he had been through, he would be ready mentally and physically. Robbie wanted to train Jake to be able to put up with abuse, which he thought was sad, but he felt it was necessary if ever he wasn't there to protect him. Robbie didn't want Jake to think that it was ok to be beaten and tortured but the way that things were going, he wasn't confident that he would always be around to save him. Anthony had threatened to kill Robbie so many times that he knew it was a real possibility. He hoped that Anthony would leave him alone for the rest of the day, but he knew that was unlikely.

Two hours had gone by and Anthony hadn't bothered the boys at all. Eventually Robbie started to think that maybe he had given up. But as soon as the thought crossed his mind, and Robbie began to think that he could relax his mind Anthony walked back up to their bedroom doorway with his evil face and dingy pants. He told Jake to put on some clothes and that he would leaving with him, but he told Robbie to just sit on the bed and be quiet. Robbie sat with a confused look on his face wondering if he was going to be left alone while Anthony took Jake somewhere. He had never been left in the house alone and he thought about how angry his mother would be if she knew that Anthony was about to do that. Jake had begun to put on his shoes and was also feeling anxious about what was happening. He said, "I don't want to go with him by myself, where is he taking me?" Robbie replied, "I don't know, but I will be ok. He isn't going to do anything to you." As soon as Jake finished getting dressed, Anthony told him to go outside and wait. After Jake went outside, Anthony came back into Robbie's room and closed the door, locking it behind him. He said, "Stand up. I told you that it wasn't over, didn't I?" Robbie didn't speak, but he stood up as instructed. Anthony walked over to the closet, opened it up, and said, "You want to be nosey, big and bad like you run shit around here? Get your ass in the here and stay in here until I get back!" Robbie went into the closet and Anthony closed the door, propping something against it so that he was locked inside. As Anthony walked way he heard him say "Don't try to get out because I will know, and I will beat the life out of your little ass if that happens! You are about to learn who the damn king is around here, this is your first day in jail nigga!" He slammed the door then Robbie heard him walk down the house and out the front door.

It was pitch dark inside the closet and very quiet. Robbie could hear his heart beating and felt himself beginning to panic. He looked around trying to see light but there was none. He didn't know what to do so he started pushing against the door to see if he could get it to open but it didn't move. Once it dawned on him that he was trapped in there he began to scream "Hey!! Somebody help! Let me out! Please!" he screamed again and again but nobody could hear him. Robbie hit and kicked at the door, nothing worked, and nobody was coming to let him out. He knew then that he would be stuck there until Anthony and Jake came back. He tried to calm himself by closing his eyes and thinking about Grace's smile but that wasn't working either. Robbie opened his eyes and still saw only darkness, it was hot in there and sweat started to run down his forehead. He thought to himself, "You can do this, be strong, nothing is going to get you." Time went by and it felt like it two hours had gone by and he was still in there alone. He had given up on screaming a long time ago and sat with his back against the wall. Suddenly, Robbie felt something touch his side and he screamed and started to swing his arms, causing the clothes that had been hanging in the closet to fall down around him.

Anthony had been strategic with this particular punishment. He wanted Robbie to feel like dying and giving up, he was trying to break him mentally. Robbie was determined to not give him that satisfaction, so he decided that maybe the best way for him to get through this was to try to sleep to make the time pass. He rocked himself back and forth thinking of the way that his mother used to rock him when he was smaller, but this wasn't working. He tried to lean back and just relax but it was too quiet, so quiet that it magnified his anxiety, so he started to scream for help again. He beat on the door, screaming, "Help me! Get me out of here! Please help me!" He thought he heard things crawling, but he couldn't see what they were, then something fell on him and crawled down his shirt. Robbie yelled, and screamed, hitting his shirt trying to get it off of him. He took the shirt off and started shaking it out, hitting it against the closet door. Robbie didn't know whether he had killed the creepy crawly or if it was still in there with him. It could have been a spider, roach, ant, or ghost. All he knew was that he wasn't going to last much longer if he couldn't get out of that closet. Robbie thought to himself, "I am going to kill Anthony, I hate him, I am going to shoot him!" Tears ran down his face, he had to use the bathroom, and knew that he might have to relieve himself in there if they didn't come back soon. Finally, Robbie heard the door open and footsteps heading towards the room. He knew it was Anthony because he'd gone accustomed to listening to him walk. Robbie didn't hear Jake though which worried him. The footsteps got closer to his room, then the door opened, and the walking stopped. Robbie knew that he couldn't show any weakness, so he got himself together as if nothing was wrong and sat there, waiting for Anthony to open the door. If he would have seen Robbie in a panic or going crazy he might have kept him in there even longer. But Robbie figured that if he opened the door and he was just sitting like nothing was wrong he might let him out and find another way to torture him. It was really quiet for a moment like Anthony might have been trying to listen to see if Robbie was crying or trying to get out, but he didn't move.

Robbie heard Anthony walk to the bed and recognized Jake's snoring as he laid him down. Knowing that Jake had fallen asleep after wherever they had been helped to ease his mind a bit as he'd been worried that Anthony had done something to him. The room, outside the closet, was still quiet so Robbie knew that Anthony was still listening to see if he'd make any noises. He was trying to decide whether or not he should say something or stay quiet. He decided to stand up and Anthony heard him and opened the door to see Robbie standing there as if nothing was wrong. Anthony frowned at him, put his index finger on Robbie's forehead and whispered, "You a man now huh? This was your test and you failed it. Trying to be big and bad is going to get you fucked up little nigga, sit your ass back down!" He pushed Robbie back down to the floor and closed the door. Robbie felt defeated and was re-thinking his strategy. Now he wondered if maybe he should have been yelling and screaming for help so that Anthony could feel powerful. Robbie thought to himself, "Boy, was I wrong. Dammit, what is he going to do now?" Robbie didn't know what Anthony wanted or expected from him. He didn't hear Jake's snoring anymore because Anthony took him out of the room. Robbie began to prepare his mind for the worse. Anthony walked back into the room, opened the closet door and told Robbie to put on pants and a long-sleeved shirt. It was already hot in the house, so Robbie wondered what Anthony was up to. He put on the clothes that he was instructed to wear, all while Anthony glared at him hatefully. Once he was fully dressed, Anthony said, "I don't like your little punk ass, you are never going to be a man do you understand me?" Robbie didn't reply, which seemed to make Anthony angrier. He slammed the door closed and slapped Robbie in the back of the head so hard that he fell face first and hit his forehead on the floor. He just laid there, he didn't cry because he didn't want to show Anthony that he was afraid. Suddenly he grabbed Robbie by the shirt and pulled him up off of the floor saying, "Get your fucking ass up, I said you will never be a man do you understand me?" Robbie still refused to speak, so Anthony responded by digging his knuckle into the side of his rib cage, pressing so hard that Robbie felt as if he was about to pass out from the pain. But Robbie was in a place mentally where he had decided that nothing Anthony did to him would force him to say that he would never be a man. Even if that meant that Anthony would kill him. The pain intensified, and Anthony said, "Answer me boy or I am going to kill your little ass in here today!" Robbie was in so much pain that he wanted to give in, but he still refused to acknowledge what Anthony was saying. He knew that one day he would be a real man like his mother had always told him, so he started smiling at Anthony. And looked him in his eyes to finally say, "No sir." Anthony stopped digging into his side then and slapped him across the face three times shouting, "Who the fuck are you talking to little nigga? You done lost your fucking mind! You are one crazy little nigga! I knew that you were a demon child I am about to fuck your punk ass up since you want to laugh and shit!" He walked to the closet door, with a wild look on his face and said, "Get your motherfucking ass back in here!" Robbie walked into the closet and went back to sitting like he was before they'd come back home. Anthony left the closet door open this time and walked out of the room. Robbie just sat and wondered about what was coming next. He'd been made to put on winter clothes and it was nowhere near winter time.

Robbie felt like he'd won a battle of wills by smiling through the latest round of torture. He knew that he'd been able to make Anthony feel like he was losing control by not giving in to what he'd done to him. Anthony was rambling and looking for something in his room while mumbling to himself angrily. Robbie tried to mentally prepare for the next phase of war and started to pray, asking God to protect his family should he not survive. He wasn't confident that he'd make it through the end of the day, so he ran out of the room to find Jake to tell him that he loved him. He found Jake still sleeping, he was lying on a bed in the girls' room. Robbie quickly hugged him, told him that he loved him and apologized for leaving him, then he ran back to his room to take his place in the closet. He felt strongly at this point that if he was going to go out, he would go out fighting with everything that he had until his last breath. He took deep breaths in and out, rocked himself back and forth, clenched his fists tight and prepared to bite if need be in order to leave evidence on Anthony to show he'd fought back. Robbie heard Anthony walking towards the room and felt his heart pounding in his chest. He came to the door and Robbie noticed that he had an electric heater in his hand. He shook his head no to signal that whatever he was about to do would not go as he planned. Anthony grinned as he plugged it up, turning it on high and said, "You better not touch his fucking heater nigga, it better stay on and your ass is going to stay in here with it and your clothes better stay on!" He slammed the door and walked to his out as it dawned on Robbie that Anthony intended to burn him up in the room.

Robbie sat on the bed, after an hour had gone by, he still didn't hear a sound from Anthony or Jake. He was drenched in sweat, and he had to use the bathroom, so he started screaming, "Hey I need to theme the bathroom! Open the door! I have to pee!" Anthony came running down the hall stood at the door and said, "Boy shut the hell up! Piss on yourself! You are not getting out of this motherfucking room!" Robbie replied, "I gotta pee really bad and it's too hot in here let me out!" Anthony laughed and said, "That's a good one but you are not getting out of this room so piss on yourself if you have to and die from heat exhaustion I don't give a fuck you are not coming out!" Robbie was feeling desperate, he had sweat pouring down his face, he was thirsty, hungry, and his bladder was beginning to hurt so he started punching and kicking the door screaming, "Let me out! I am going to tell his mama when she come home!" He knew that Anthony would open the door when he said that, and he was right. The door swung open and Anthony said, "What the fuck did you just say? You are going to do what?" Robbie stood as close to the door as possible so that he could feel the cool air come in and it felt so good. Anthony had no clue what he was doing, Robbie just wanted him to open the door so that he could get some relief from the heat. He had been willing to say anything in order to get some cool air, even if it resulted in another beating. Robbie wiped the sweat off his face and said, "I have to pee, and I am hungry can I please use the bathroom and have something to eat?" Anthony put his foot on Robbie's chest, pushing him down with his foot and said, "Nigga if you ever say anything to your mama I will kill you and her, fuck that shit I will kill all ya'll dumb motherfuckers!" This enraged Robbie, he was the protector of his family and if anybody threatened him, they would feel his wrath. He got up off of the floor and said, "Why would you do that to them and why did you call them dumb? They are not dumb!?" Robbie didn't care anymore, enough was enough and he was tired being afraid. Anthony grabbed him by the neck, lifting him up off of the ground and said, "As long as you are alive you better never question me nigga, I don't have to answer shit you ask me!" Robbie was kicking to try to get Anthony to loosen his grip. He was losing his breath and feeling like he was being strangled, finally Anthony threw him down on the floor and said, "You will stay your little ass in here until I say you can come out!" He walked out of the room and slammed the door. Robbie was still struggling to get his breathing back on track, but it was the first time that he had stood up to Anthony and even though he was nearly killed, it felt good.

Achy, sore and hot, Robbie went back to his bed where he sat for hours. He was seating so bad that he thought he might pass out. He'd accepted that Anthony wouldn't let him out to use the bathroom, so he urinated in the vent, where the air conditioner and heat would normally come through. He hadn't wanted to pee on himself, he was already drenched because of the sweat and he didn't want to give Anthony the satisfaction of further humiliating him. It was getting dark and Robbie was struggling to survive, he hadn't seen Jake, he hadn't eaten all day. Finally, Anthony walked to the door, opened it and looked at Robbie, grinning, he said "Yeah, little nigga you weak now huh? Go in that kitchen and eat that hot dog on the table, then come back and get out of them clothes and put you on your night clothes. When your mama get here you better keep your mouth shut, you better act like everything was good and like you had a great day today you hear me?" At this point Robbie didn't care what Anthony said, he was just ready to eat, and get out of his sweaty clothes. He replied, "Yes sir", and went to the kitchen where he saw the most awful looking hot dog he'd ever seen in his life. He picked it up, looked at it, the bun was stale, the hot dog was cold, it looked like Anthony had done something to it, it had holes in it and it was dirty like it had been rolled on the floor. Robbie didn't know what else he might have done to it, he might have been trying to poison him, so he looked around to make sure Anthony wasn't watching, then he threw it in the trash. After doing that Robbie wondered if Anthony might come and check to see if he had eaten it and it dawned on him that he might check the garbage can. So, he quickly took the hotdog out of the trash and decided to try to feed it to Anthony's dog. Robbie quietly snuck to the back door and ran out towards the old car where the dog was tied up. It was a mangy old German Shepard that nobody interacted with so Robbie knew he had to be quick so that it wouldn't bark at him. He through the hotdog towards him and took off running back towards the back door and into the kitchen.

When Robbie made it back to the table, he sat down as if he had just finished eating, the dog was still barking so Anthony came into the kitchen and looked out the window to see what he was barking at. Robbie hoped and prayed that the dog would stop barking soon and he hoped that Anthony wouldn't go out there and see any remnants of the hotdog. Anthony was starting to walk towards the door and finally the dog stopped barking. He turned around, looked at Robbie saying "Why are you still sitting there? You don't get no more food and you better had eaten it all." Anthony did what Robbie had expected him to and walked over to look in the trash to make sure he hadn't thrown it away. When he saw that there was nothing there he started smiling like he had gotten away with his plan and asked, "Was it good boy?" Robbie responded, "Yes sir." Anthony told him to go to his room and get out of those clothes. Robbie noticed that Anthony had already taken the heater out of his room, he put on fresh clothes as instructed but he was so hungry and dehydrated that he felt weak. He hoped that since Anthony was trying to cover his tracks that meant that Grace would be home soon, and he'd find some relief. The bedroom was still a little warm, but he was sure that by the time his mom got home it would have been cooled off.

After a while, Jake came in the room and seemed upset, so Robbie asked him, "What's wrong with you why are you looking at me like that?" He replied, "Anthony told me not to talk to you right now and I don't like him for that." Robbie replied, "It will ok brother, don't be mad everything will be ok, just go get in your bed and let's wait for mother to come home." He sat and stared at Robbie with a sad look on his face. Robbie could see that Jake felt sorry for him, but he knew that he couldn't do anything to change what was happening. It bothered Robbie to have Jake feeling so sad for him, so he knew he had to be strong to give him something to look up to. Even though he was going through hell he didn't want Jake stressed and worrying. After waiting for a while, the boys heard Grace's car pulling up and they were so happy. She'd been gone all day long.

Anthony came back to the room and gave Robbie a threatening look as if to signal that he better not say a word, then he went back to his room. Grace and the girls came into the house and Robbie could smell food. He got so excited, it smelled so good that his mouth began to water. It was McDonald's! Jake and Robbie were thrilled, it was so rare that they ate fast food this was really a treat. They stayed in their room and waited to be called and suddenly the girls came running down the hall screaming, "Mama said come and get your food before it gets cold!" The boys took off running to the kitchen. Robbie was thinking that God had finally answered his prayers. He hadn't eaten all day and now he'd be able to eat food from his favorite restaurant. Both boys plopped down in their chairs and waited for their mother to tell them which bag of food theirs was. Grace was in the room with Anthony talking about something and Robbie was getting impatient.

Soon she came around the corner, into the kitchen, walked up to them both and said, "Hey my handsome boys, did ya'll have fun today?" They both looked at each other as if they'd been coached and responded, "Yes ma'am." She looked at them as if something wasn't right, then she said, "Oh really, so what did ya'll do today?" Robbie felt himself start to panic, Anthony hadn't told him what to tell their mom and he hadn't done anything other than be tortured. Luckily Jake started to talk about their fun filled day, he said, "We went to the park, played on the merry go round, we went to the store and got some ice cream, then we went to our cousin's house and played with their dog, and came back home to wait for you." Anthony was slick, he knew that he had to do something so that if Grace had asked them about what they'd done, one of them would be able to answer. He'd decided to take Jake to have fun and then scare him into not blowing their cover. And he also knew that he'd be able to beat Robbie and get away with it.

Grace looked at Robbie and said, "So did you like doing all of that?" Robbie put his head down and then Anthony walked into kitchen to the refrigerator, so he responded, "Yes ma'am I really had fun, especially with the dog and at the park." She smiled and said, "Good that's what I wanted to hear." Lying to Grace made Robbie feel sick to his stomach, he wanted to tell her what was going on, but he believed that Anthony would kill them all just like he'd threatened. Grace was asking too many questions and Robbie didn't want her to keep prying or it was going to end badly. He finished his food, got up from the table and I passed gas to create a distraction, when this happened everyone started laughing. This definitely changed the mood, Grace was so tickled, she said, "Boy you are crazy with your stanking ass self!" All of the children were just laughing until their stomachs hurt. Robbie was laughing so hard that he passed gas again and Grace said, "Boy stop doing that before you shit on yourself, you need to go and check your draws because you stank!" They were all having a great time laughing and Robbie could see Anthony standing in the corner glaring at him, obviously upset that he was having a good time. Then he noticed Grace watching Anthony to see his reaction could see Grace looking at him out of the corner of her eyes to see his reaction, he was the only one not laughing and having a good time. Robbie knew that if he continued to be patient, eventually Grace would figure him out.

CHAPTER
22

It was tough, but Robbie knew he had to be smart and go about doing things the right way. Anthony left the kitchen in a hurry, he didn't want to be a part of their family. Grace sat in the kitchen with the children and watched them eat their food, she stared at Robbie as if she knew that something was wrong. Robbie tried to avoid looking into her eyes, she was watching his interaction with his siblings and listening to everything that they were saying. Jake had no idea what was going on.

The girls were talking about how good of a time they had, and Jake was telling them how good of a time he had, what he didn't realize was that when he was talking about what he did he never included Robbie in the story, so a look of concern spread across Grace's face. She stood up, went to close the kitchen door, then walked back to sit down. She stopped the children from talking, put Jake on her lap and said, "Where was your brother at today because you never said anything about him being with you and Anthony? When I first asked you both how was your day, the both of you looked at each other so why did you do that?" Robbie was thinking, in that moment, "Oh shit it's about to go down!" Jake put his head down so Robbie tried to speak for him, but Grace cut him off and said, "I am talking to him not you, you shut up and you wait your turn to talk when I tell you that you can talk." Robbie replied, "Yes ma'am." Grace knew something wasn't right and she figured out that the boys were lying to her, so she was pissed off because she hated liars. She stood Jake up in front of her and asked him again, "Where was your brother when ya'll were gone out?" Now one thing for sure that was scarier than Anthony was Grace, she was one woman that you didn't want to piss off. Jake knew this, so he had no choice but to tell the truth and Robbie didn't want to risk having his head knocked off. Jake started to cry so Grace grabbed his cheeks and asked him, "Why are you crying boy? Why are you not answering my damn question?" He replied, "Because I am scared mama I don't want to get in trouble, and I don't want Robbie to get in trouble." She replied,

"Who told you that you would get in trouble if you told me something?" He pointed to the direction where her room was and said, "Him, Mr. Anthony, mama." She told Jake to go sit down and told Robbie to come over to her. Robbie was so nervous that he was shaking.

Grace put her hands on Robbie's shoulders, her hands were also shaking because she was angry, she looked at him and said, "I am only going to ask you one time before I go in there to ask him, you and your brother are not going to get in trouble, because nobody is going to touch my damn kids so you need to tell me son, where were you when Anthony and your brother were away?" He knew Grace, and the rage she could feel when it came to her kids, and so Robbie decided to tell part of the truth. He knew that if he told her the whole thing in detail, she would have gone completely off. This is what he was trying to prevent because of Anthony's threat to kill them all. Robbie could not put his family at risk, he felt that their lives were his responsibility. He looked Grace and said, "I was in my room, laying on the bed." She turned her head to the side like she always did when she gets mad and said, "Laying on the bed?" Robbie replied, "Yes ma'am." She put her hands on her hips, started pacing back and forth, and said, "Wait a minute, why was my child left at home by himself in the first fucking place? What happened son?" Robbie had to think quick fast and, in a hurry, he replied, "I didn't want my cereal because there wasn't enough milk so I threw it away and Anthony got mad and told me to go to my room." She replied, "I don't give a damn how much cereal you wasted, don't nobody leave my baby at home by himself!"

Both of the girls were shocked, the looks on their faces spoke a million words, they knew that their mother was about to take her anger to another level and they knew how bad it was for Anthony to leave Robbie all alone while he and Jake enjoyed their day. Grace told all of them to go to their rooms and close the door, she also told them not to open them until she said so. They followed her instruction and she went to her room where Anthony was, with the door closed. Robbie had a very bad feeling, so he was trying to prepare himself for the worst. Jake was laying in his bed with the pillow over his face and ears so that he couldn't hear what was going on. Robbie needed to be at the door so that he could hear everything that was happening, and the girls were as quiet as little mice. They never liked conflict or drama, so they stayed away from it, but Robbie always inserted himself into the middle of it all, being the man of the house. He felt it was his role to protect everyone. Grace's door slammed so hard that the picture in the living room fell on the floor. She had told the children to stay in their rooms, but Robbie was not about to let Anthony hurt his mother. He opened the door, went out into the living room and stood in front of their door to listen to what was happening. Robbie didn't care if he got caught, it was about making sure that Grace was safe that is all that mattered.

When Robbie put his ear to the door he heard Grace screaming at Anthony saying, "What the fuck is wrong with your dumb ass? You left my child in this fucking house all by himself and you were probably gone for a long damn time too! I should fuck you up right now nigga!" Robbie heard movement and put his hand on the door so that he could get ready to burst in and fight. Anthony said, "Get out my face, I am not playing with you just get out my face and I will leave you and your kids alone ok." Grace was breathing hard, Robbie knew it was about to go down. She replied, "Oh so they my kids now huh nigga? You wasn't saying that shit yesterday after your dumb ass was trying to work your way back up in his house bitch! I am going to stay right here in your face and if you put a hand on me I am going to fuck your ass up nigga I swear on my mama grave!" Anthony replied, "You are not going to do shit to me but get out of my face, yeah I told his little bad ass to go in that room and sit there and think about wasting food, yeah I left him here, but I came right back go and ask him!" Robbie wondered to himself, "Why did he have to lie like that?" If Grace had opened the door and asked if he had come right back, Robbie would have told her the truth because he'd been gone for hours. Grace replied, "I am not going to ask him shit! You left my fucking child in this house alone when you know he is not old enough to be here by himself!" Anthony replied, "He is old enough in his eyes, he got you wrapped around his little finger, you think that boy is an angel, you don't see the shit that I see him do, you don't be here enough to know what the hell goes down! I keep them most of the time, so I see everything! Yeah, I disciplined him, he needed it! He lucky I didn't beat his ass, the only reason why I didn't is because I have to get your permission to discipline these kids!" Robbie could not believe that Anthony was saying this when he'd literally almost killed him on numerous occasions.

Robbie was getting angrier by the minute while listening to Anthony's lies about what happened. Grace wasn't falling for any of it though, she ignored everything he was saying and got back in Anthony's face and said, "First of all my son is a great kid and you will not keep talking about his child like that. I know my child and I know he don't do none of the shit that you are saying, you are a fucking liar, and you are not his daddy. I am his mama and his daddy he don't need shit from another man in his life that is going to hurt him. And you are the one that's lucky because if you would've put your hands on my child you would've been checking into the Hotel Cemetery because I don't play about my kids!" Once Grace was fed up there was nothing that anybody could do to get her out of the frame of mind that she was in. Anthony got really quiet and then got up into Grace's face and said, "So are you threatening me? Are you motherfucking telling me that you are going to kill me?" Grace replied, "You better get the fuck out of my face and keep your fucking hands to yourself! You don't scare me nigga I hits back, and I don't give a fuck how big you are, so you best get your hands off me right now and I am not playing!" Robbie ran to his room, got Jake, and took him into the room with their sisters. Once they were all together, he whispered, "Anthony and mama are about to fight, and I am about to go in there and fight him with her, ya'll can stay here and lock the door if you want but I will be back." That got them all riled up, they were ready to jump on Anthony too in order to protect their mother. Robbie had the siblings go to the kitchen and get forks, then he told them to wait by the door for his signal. Robbie had a fork and a knife that he'd planned on using as weapons. He went back to his mother's door to listen while the other children waited in the girl's room.

Robbie's siblings were just as upset as he was about what was happening, they were ready to die or kill for their mama. He could overhear them saying to themselves, "Nobody is not going to touch our mama, we will kill them! If he hits mama, we will stab him!" They were ready, and Robbie was in position, Anthony began to scream, "You won't do shit but talk! All that fucking mouth and won't do a damn thing to me because I am the king in this mother fucker! What I say goes! I run this shit whether you pay the fucking bills or not, now sit your ass down!"

This was the side of Anthony that Grace never saw, this was his alter ego. The crazy psychotic monster that had been abusing Robbie was finally showing up. Suddenly Robbie heard his mother fall to the floor after being hit by Anthony, and she screamed, "I am going to kill you bitch! You done fucked up now and put your fucking hands on me!" This was the green light for Robbie to go in and commence to stabbing his ass! He turned and yelled for his siblings, "Come on ya'll he hitting mama!" They all came running out of the room screaming to the top of their lungs, Robbie turned the door knob and burst through the door! Anthony was on top of Grace choking and slapping her. Robbie had lost the knife as he turned the door knob, but he ran and grabbed Anthony around the neck while biting and trying to stab him with the fork! The other children had all jumped-on Anthony as well and were biting, kicking and stabbing him in his legs with the forks. He was trying his best to get them off of him, but he couldn't, he would throw one off and another came. On top of that he had Grace to deal with and when she saw them come into help her fight, she took it into another mode. Anthony was screaming, "Get your crazy ass kids off me they stabbing me with fucking forks!" They were all screaming, "Get off our mama, and don't hit our mama!" Grace was kicking him in the side and punching his face saying, "I told your ass not to put your hands on me, now you doing this in front of my kids!" She put her arm around his neck and put him in a choke hold.

Grace was country strong, so once she had gotten him off of her and gained control of him she would give him a run for his money without question! As she had him in a sleeper hold, she told the children to back up because she had him. Anthony was gasping for air, he was already out of shape because he smoked so many cigarettes, but he was to the point to where he was about to tap out. He said, "Let me go, you trying to kill me girl let me go!" Grace replied, "I told you not to fuck with me or my kids, didn't I?" Anthony replied, "I can't breathe, just let me go and I will leave!" This was the best feeling in the world to Robbie. Seeing Anthony beg for his life felt like the ultimate revenge to having been victimized by him. Robbie was smiling and looking him dead in his eyes, he didn't want Grace to stop so he said, "No mama don't stop, kill him!" He looked at Robbie, looking like a fish taking its last breaths and said, "Kill me? You going to sit here and let your son tell you to kill me?" Grace replied, "My child can say what the fuck he wants, you put your hands on me nigga I should break your fucking neck!" Robbie was loving every minute of Anthony being in pain, so he said, "Yeah mama break his neck!" Grace looked at Robbie, frowned and said, "Boy hush I got this!" Robbie replied, "Yes ma'am". She gripped Anthony's neck even stronger, then she said, "If I let you go, I want, you to leave right now or I am going to call the police." Anthony was beat, he had no energy to fight back and no reason to want to be there, so he replied, "I will leave ok just let me go and I promise I will walk straight out the door." Robbie didn't trust him at all, but he trusted Grace's instincts so if she let him go and he tried to do something crazy he knew she would handle that. Before she let him go she told Robbie to go to the closet and get the shotgun that was in the back of the closet. Robbie ran as fast as he could to grab it. Anthony said, "Oh it's like that? You are going to pull out a gun on me after all of the shit we have been through?" Grace replied, "Nigga I don't trust you anymore, so yes I am going to have my gun right by my side ready to blast your ass if you try something crazy with my kids in the house!"

Grace was not playing, she was so serious, and Anthony knew it, Anthony replied, "You are wrong for this, you know I wouldn't hurt your kids, you started this shit with me, but I will leave you don't have to worry about me anymore!" Grace replied, "Good, you can come back and get your shit once you have calmed down and I tell you that you can come!" Robbie opened the closet door and there was Grace's shotgun, he picked it up and sat it right down beside her. Grace slowly let Anthony go and quickly grabbed her weapon and pointed it straight at Anthony's back. Anthony had gotten up gasping for air, when he turned around he seemed shocked that Grace had the gun pointed straight into his chest. He looked at the gun then looked at her and said, "You pulled a weapon on me, you should've never done that, you should've gone ahead and used it." Grace yelled, "Leave my motherfucking house right now!" Robbie's heart was racing, he could see in her eyes that she was done with Anthony completely, there was no coming back. He walked out of the door and as he was walking he said, "That was a very big mistake, I will be back." Grace replied, "You were the fucking mistake and you better not show up at his house without my permission!"

CHAPTER
23

Robbie could not believe what had just taken place, he'd known that it would only be a matter of time until shit hit the fan, but he didn't expect it to happen that fast. Anthony was walking towards the street talking trash to Grace, but she didn't pay him any attention, she just slammed the door behind him. Then she walked back to her room, with a dazed look on her face and sat on the bed. The children stood at the door and staring at her when she noticed them standing there she began to cry and rocked herself back and forth. She put her hands on her face and the tears were flowing. The children hated to see their mother cry, so they began to cry too. Tori walked up to Grace and said, "Mama don't cry please mama don't cry everything is going to be ok." She looked back at her and said, "I know baby, mama know, we all are going to be ok." All of them went up and began to hug her and she hugged them all back and said, "It's time that I just focus on me and my babies, ya'll don't have to worry about going through this again, I am so sorry that I put ya'll through this, but it won't happen anymore." They all said ok and continued to hug her, emotions were running high after having just fought to protect their mother from Anthony.

Robbie was shocked that with all Anthony had threatened to do, nobody had been seriously hurt or killed during that fight. He wanted to tell Grace everything that Anthony had done to him, but he felt that it wasn't the right time, so he decided to keep it to himself for the time being. Anthony was never coming back to be with Grace Robbie knew it for a fact this time, Grace was completely done with that monster so there was no need to tell her anything. Robbie knew Anthony would need to come back for his belongings and he hoped there would be no issues, but he wondered if things could end that easily.

Anthony had been beaten up by Grace and the children, so he'd lost his power. He was no king, he was a nobody trying to be somebody, and he didn't deserve to be a damn thing. He was childish and petty, so Robbie felt like he Anthony still had a game plan especially since

it wasn't over. Grace didn't know the version of him that Ro.

there were multiple aspects of his personality that she'd never seen

that day. He was capable of anything, Robbie thought of the many time

he'd threatened to kill them all, and knew they'd have to be prepared for

it. Robbie watched his mother crying and it made him angry, he took her

by the hand and said, "Mama I love you, I don't want nothing to happen

to you, what if he come back and try to do something to us, what are we

going to do?" She replied, "Son he is not that crazy, he want people to

think he is crazy but when he comes back to get his stuff, everything will

be ok." Robbie knew that Anthony was a psycho, and capable of doing

some really bad and devilish things. But he responded "Ok" the continued

to hug on her with his siblings. Eventually Grace calmed down and got

herself together, and although Robbie expected him to come back, he

didn't. Grace asked them to help her clean up the mess that was made while

fighting off Anthony. All of the children pitched in to help her clean up,

and things began to feel like they were back to normal.

Robbie thought back to when he used to worry about Grace taking

Anthony back when he would mess up. This time felt different. There was

no tension in the air, there was freedom, and he felt like he could breathe

a bit easier. He looked over at his siblings who were all smiling and staring

at Grace, as she smiled back at them. In her eyes, Robbie could see that

she was sorry, and she promised that they'd never be in this position again.

No more drama, beatings, negativity, abuse, it was the best feeling in the

world. It was like God had taken the weight off of Robbie's shoulders

and he could be kid and again. He thought about going outside to play,

spending the night at friends' houses, playing with toys, and living life

with no worries. He had been praying for this since Anthony had come

into their lives. The hate that Robbie had for Anthony was deep, he'd

often found himself fantasizing about ways to kill him. Robbie knew that

it would take some time to get past everything that had happened to him

but part of him suspected that the experiences he'd had would haunt him

for the rest of his life. He tried to embrace the moment and be happy,

maybe once Anthony's belongings were out of the house he'd feel even

better. Grace told the children to go into their rooms and put on their night clothes then she invited them to sleep in the bed with her. They were all so excited.

They ran to their rooms to change, and Grace came by their rooms to tell them to brush their teeth, but she stopped mid-sentence and said, "What is that smell, it smell like piss!" Robbie's eyes got really big, and he replied, "I don't know mama." She said, "Did one of ya'll pee in the bed?" The boys both said, "No Ma'am". She went to their beds and smelled the covers, opened the closet and started looking around in the closet but she couldn't find where the smell was coming from. Of course, Robbie knew where the smell was coming from, but he couldn't tell her that he'd had to urinate in the vents because Anthony had locked him in the room all day. So, he continued to get dressed, hoping that she wouldn't figure out where the smell was coming from. She finally walked out of the room, mumbling to herself, "I don't know where in the hell that smell is coming from, but we are going to give this house a good cleaning soon and get all the stank and evil spirits out here." The children said, "Ok mama!" then they went with her to get in bed. The four children piled into their mother's bed waiting for Grace to get in with them. Then the arguing began amongst them about who would get to sleep next to her, so they decided to play "Paper, Rock, Scissors" to settle the argument. The girls won so one slept in front and the other slept in back of Grace, Jake slept on one side of Grace's foot and Robbie slept at the other.

They were bundled up in the bed like a bunch of Vienna sausages, but they didn't mind, they'd all just wanted to be near their mother. Before Grace turned the lights out she gave them each a big hug and a kiss then said, "Ya'll are my four munchkins and I thank God for each and every one of you! I love ya'll with all my heart and things are going to get better I promise." The children replied in unison, "We love you too mama!" As Robbie tried to fall asleep, he thought about what an amazing feeling it was to finally be a real family like he'd wanted it to be years ago. It was hard to believe that it was finally happening, he was so excited and ready to live a normal life. Everyone was asleep but him, he couldn't seem to completely relax because it felt like he needed to watch out and listen for Anthony in case he tried to come back. Robbie's mind was plagued with various scenarios of Anthony coming in to kill them as they slept. But as the hours went by the only thing he heard was his mother and siblings snoring like hibernating bears and kicking him in his side. Robbie eventually drifted off to sleep.

A few hours had gone by when all of a sudden Grace's alarm went off and scared them all to death. They jumped up looking around at each other, everybody was accounted for but Grace. Where had she gone? Robbie thought to himself. But then he smelled bacon and knew that she was in the kitchen cooking that good ole country breakfast. He jumped down and ran into the kitchen to give Grace a big hug and tell her good morning. She looked different for some reason, she seemed happy and that's how he wanted to see her. This meant the world to him; their family didn't have much but they had each other. Grace told them all to go and wash their faces, brush their teeth, then come back to sit at the table. Robbie quickly did as she instructed and got back to the table to watch her cook, dance and sing. Suddenly she turned around, saw him staring at her and she smiled saying, "Hey handsome what you looking at?" That made him smile and blush, he responded "I am looking at the most beautiful woman in the world, you mama!" She replied, "Why thank you my sweet baby!" Just to see Grace not worrying or thinking about Anthony was an amazing feeling, the other children sat down beside him to get ready to stuff their bellies.

Grace was cooking the biggest breakfast that they had ever seen! She had cheese grits, bacon, sausages, cheese eggs, pancakes, and homemade biscuits! Robbie was amazed, if this was any indication of what life without Anthony would be like, he could only imagine what the future would hold. None of the children were used to their mother being so happy and cooking so much food. As she finished up and made everyone's plates she said, "After ya'll finish eating, I want you put you some clothes on for church." They looked at each other, not knowing what to make of all this. Their mother was cooking breakfast, singing, smiling, in a good mood and they would be going to church? It all felt unreal, Robbie had to pinch himself and see he was dreaming. He could not believe that they were going to church. They all loved going when they got a chance to but Grace usually worked so much that it rarely happened. Grace continued talking and she explained to them that it was time for a change and that they needed to get back to being a family and going to church. They needed Jesus, the family was broken and needed to be patched up the right way.

The monster was no longer around to bring negativity into their lives, so it was all positive vibes and it felt good. Everyone finished their food, helped clean the kitchen and hurried to get dressed for church. Ever the skeptic, Robbie felt like everything seemed too good to be true, like at any moment, something bad was going to happen and they would be back to square one. He tried to get that negative thought off of his mind, but things usually happened the way he expected them to. He went through every scenario that he could think of. His anxiety warping his thoughts as usual. He wondered, "What if Anthony came in when they were least expecting him and killed them, or what if he was waiting outside right now for them to come outside so that he could shoot them? Or what if he tricked Grace into meeting him somewhere alone?" Anything was possible with Anthony, Grace didn't seem to think that he was capable of doing such things, but Robbie knew better. He tried in vain not to let these thoughts bother him, but he couldn't let them go. At this point in Robbie's life, his nerves were so frayed that he almost always expected the worst.

CHAPTER
24

Everyone was dressed and ready to go so Grace told them all to head out to the car. When she came outside she looked amazing! She was wearing a beautiful black dress, she had lipstick on, and her bible in her hand. Robbie thought she was absolutely gorgeous and the children all told her how pretty she was when she got into the car. Grace turned the car on, put her shades on and said, "I'm going to tell ya'll right now, don't act up in church because if you do I am going to beat your asses right in front of the church." They all knew that Grace wasn't playing she was dead serious, as beautiful as she was. They arrived right before service was starting and it was packed inside which made Robbie happy because he liked to sit in the back. He didn't like when the church members used to look their way as they walked inside. It always felt to Robbie like they were staring at him and his family.

As soon as he saw a seat in the back and started walk towards it, Grace redirected them to seats in the very front of the church right where the pastor's pulpit was located. Robbie scowled angrily at the idea of having to walk past all of those people to get to the front of the church. He could feel the eyes burning a hole in his face, so he returned their stares with a mean look. Service went on as expected, the praise and worship singers began. Before they could even sit down, Grace was in tears. The words in the song that they were singing brought her to her knees. Robbie was mortified, he wanted to sink into the floor because all of the attention was on them. He felt that when Grace became emotional like that people would automatically think that they were troubled kids. Robbie knew that he needed to get over that way of thinking because he knew that not all churches were like that. And yes, they were a troubled family, but he didn't want anyone else...strangers to know that. Church seemed like a bunch of nosey, busybodies. People started to come over to hold Grace and pray for her. The pastor was speaking in tongues and people were crying all over the place. Grace was screaming and yelling, "Help me Lord, get the devil out my life, out my family, out of me!" Robbie put his head down and tried not to notice the whole church looking at them. Finally, it was over and Grace had calmed down but Robbie could feel her trembling. He knew they needed God, for sure.

After the pastor preached his sermon and service was over, Grace wanted to stay around and talk to the people that she knew, Robbie was ready to go so he walked to the car. He got to the car, alone, he just needed to breathe so he just sat there and waited for his mom and siblings. The wind was blowing lightly so he closed his eyes and let it blow him into another world. It felt good to be free at last. Grace and the rest of the children made it to the car, got in and put their seat belts on. She cranked up the car, put her shades on, and said, "When we get home I am going to cook Sunday dinner and then we are going to give that house a really good cleaning." The children all said, "Ok Mama, yes ma'am." Robbie said, "Mama what are we going to do with Anthony's stuff?" She replied, "Just let me worry about that son, if anything I will put it all in the living room until he comes to get it." He replied, "Yes ma'am." It made him smile just to know that Anthony's belongings wouldn't be there anymore.

The trip home was like a breath of fresh air, Grace was playing her favorite jams, and the children were all singing, dancing, and having a great time. They were a real family again, Grace had finally realized that she didn't need a man in order for them to be a family which is what he'd wanted for years. Robbie hoped that she would take her time and focus on them and herself. He didn't want her to get hurt anymore because she had gone through so much pain that she deserved to be free from stress and relationship worries. When they pulled up to the house it felt different, like there was a darkness hovering over it. Robbie had a very bad feeling about it and was hoping that Anthony wasn't inside waiting for them, so he wanted to be the first one to go inside. He was willing to risk himself by going in first to give Grace and his siblings the chance to escape. They all sat in the car for a moment and Grace stared at the house like she was in a daze. Robbie wondered if she was thinking the way he was, so he asked her, "Mama what are you thinking?" She replied, "I think it's time that we find another place to live what ya'll think?" They all replied, "Yes mama let's move!" She looked at them, smiled and said, "Next week I am going to start looking for a new place. This house just don't feel right anymore. I am supposed to start my new job next week too, so I will be making more money." They were all so happy to hear that she was even thinking about moving. Everyone cheered and celebrated so loud and hard that Grace had to tell them to calm it down and act like they had some sense. Robbie asked Grace for the key so that he could go and unlock the door, he stuck the key inside and before he turned it to open the door he looked back and said, "If anything happen to me I want ya'll to run but remember that I will always love ya'll." Grace replied, "Boy open that damn door, nothing is going to happen to you, got me cursing and I just got out of church." Robbie said, "Yes ma'am, but what if Anthony is inside waiting for us mama then what?" She replied, "That man is not inside of his house, he is not that crazy, now go on in that house before I whoop your red butt boy." It really bothered Robbie that Grace thought Anthony was not that crazy because he knew first hand that he was beyond crazy, but he went ahead and opened the door.

When they walked in, everything looked the same, there was no Anthony. Grace seemed to be fine, she acted as if nothing was wrong, but Robbie knew that she was hurting. She just needed to be strong for the kids and deal with the consequences. She still loved Anthony and love was something that she took seriously, although she knew she was making the right decision, it was difficult. Robbie tried to understand the ins and outs of love, but he couldn't wrap his head around it all. He went to his room to change clothes and get ready to help with Sunday dinner. After he was done, he went to the kitchen where Grace was and asked her, "Mama what are we having for dinner?" She replied, "You know I have to do it up for my babies, we are having Barbeque Chicken, Smothered Pork chops, rice and Gravy, Cabbage, Macaroni and Cheese, Homemade Cornbread, and Punch."

Robbie's mouth was watering already just from hearing her tell him what was on the menu. The family rarely had large meals like this, so he knew that Grace was feeling good. Robbie loved to eat, and he was the biggest fan of Grace's cooking. Every time he ate her food, he would dance and sing until she told him to shut up. Robbie asked if she needed help and she replied that she was ok, she just wanted the children to go in the living room and relax until she was finished. Robbie headed to the living room to watch television with his siblings, they decided to watch

'Sandford and Son'. Everything was going perfectly, Robbie felt a little paranoid because he thought that every sound he heard was Anthony. Knowing that he would need to come back for his stuff really had Robbie worried. Every time that the kids would laugh out loud he would get angry and frightened. Eventually he was able to calm down and relax to watch his siblings enjoy themselves and be kids. He heard Grace in the kitchen singing, dancing, and a feeling of happiness overwhelmed him. Robbie was smiling but the feeling brought tears to his eyes, just reflecting on everything leading up to this point. The food was smelling so good, he was ready for Grace to call them and say that the food was done. As she cooked the food, she periodically came into the living room to sit with them and get some laughs in, then she would go back to check on the food. Finally, Grace shouted, "Ya'll come and eat!" They jumped up and sprinted to the kitchen to sit down. The table looked like a dinner from a commercial, they were about to have a feast. Robbie started dancing immediately and Grace turned on the kitchen sink saying, "Ya'll come wash your hands and sit at the table, I am about to fix your plates." The children washed their hands and sat down at the table. Everything was beautiful and cooked to perfection Robbie couldn't take it much longer, he was rocking back and forth waiting for Grace to tell them to eat. The plates were prepared, the children said the grace and it was show time.

The food was so good that nobody said one word the entire time, all you could hear was the sound of the family enjoying their meal. Grace told them to eat as much as they wanted and that they did. Robbie was the last one at the table, he ate so much food that he could barely walk. After he finished eating he wobbled into the living room where everyone else was, Grace was in the middle of the couch laid back snoring, the girls were on each side of her looking like stuffed piñatas and Jake was on the floor in between Grace's legs half asleep. They had over done it but that meal was well deserved, it had been a long time coming Robbie decided to join in on the family nap. He found a seat on the couch, kissed Grace on the forehead and laid back to watch television and doze off. About an hour or so later, Grace woke up to tell them all to get ready to clean the house. Robbie was excited about cleaning, it was always a good time with his mother because she would put on the music and they would have fun with it as a family. The best part about it was that there was no Anthony to spoil their good time.

Grace turned on her music and they all ran into the kitchen where she was washing dishes, the album she was playing was the Michael Jackson "Thriller" album. Michael Jackson was Robbie's hero, he wanted to be just like him, and he had the glove, the glittery coat, and the pants. He also wanted to dance like him so when she put that album on, Robbie ran to his room to put his outfit on and came back to the kitchen to do his Michael Jackson dance. Grace separated them all, she told the girls to go and start cleaning in their room and the boys to start cleaning their room. After that, she wanted them to go to the living room to finish up in there. The music was loud, and the family was grooving. The girls were singing along to "Billie Jean" with Grace while Jake and Robbie tried to "moonwalk" as they cleaned their rooms. It was priceless, they were all grooving to the beats and getting down. The children all finished and met in the living room to finish up together. Grace went to change the music, looking through her records, she said, "Ya'll know what time it is!" The children all looked at each other and replied, "The Soul Train Line!" Grace smiled and put the record on play. The soul train line was how they finished up when cleaning the house, it was the grand finale. The song that Grace decided to play was "The Men All Pause" by the group Klymaxx and this was one of Robbie's favorite songs.

He was ready to really get down! Everyone formed the lines and Tori went through doing her dance, then Laura went through, but she was so busy laughing that she was barely grooving to the beat. Then came Jake who was smooth with his dancing skills, snapping his fingers and popping as he moved. Next it was Robbie's turn to show off for his mom, she loved watching him dance. He got funky with it, imitating James Brown moves, the funky chicken, and the moonwalk, as Grace and the other children laughed and watched. Next was Grace's turn which was what all of the children had been looking forward to. Grace could really dance, she was known for turning out parties and it was amazing to see her get down with the get down!

She came through the soul train line and dropped it like it was hot then came up and did the robot, Grace was so cool and smooth with her moves, the kids watched in awe. Everyone had a great time cleaning up and it was time to get ready for bed, so Grace said, "We are done my babies, I had fun but now it's time for ya'll to go to bed because you have school tomorrow." None of them wanted the night to end so they were all disappointed that it was bedtime. Robbie wasn't sleepy, so he tried to come up with a reason to stay up a little longer. He said, "Mama, can I help you finish up your room please?" Grace responded, "No son that isn't going to work this time, take your butt to bed I will clean my own room." Robbie replied, "Yes ma'am" and slowly walked to his room with his head down.

Robbie missed Grace already and she was right there in the same house. The children got ready for bed, put on their night clothes then went to kiss Grace good night. Robbie was the last one to say good night to her, she knew he was sad and just wanted to spend more time with her, so she whispered in his ear, "When they go to sleep you can sneak back to my room and help me clean up ok?" Suddenly, the biggest smile spread across his face, and he quietly replied, "Yes ma'am." Robbie went to his room and laid in bed to pretend like he was going to sleep so his siblings wouldn't know their plan. He said good night to everyone, but Jake kept trying to sneak and talk to him about him about the awesome day they'd had. Robbie just tried to get him to go to sleep because he wanted to get back to Grace's room to help her. After about thirty minutes Jake finally went to sleep so Robbie quietly got up, eased out of the bed and tip toed out of the room. As he walked by the girls' room he noticed that they were both fast asleep, so the coast was clear. Then he stopped in his tracks when he heard sniffling coming from Grace's room. She was crying again, sitting on the floor, in front of her bed.

They'd just had such a good time, he couldn't understand why she would be sitting there crying. It made him wonder if she had been faking her happiness the whole day. Robbie knew that she was sad and still hurt by what Anthony had done. She had hoped and prayed that they would end up together happily ever after, but things hadn't panned out that way and it crushed her. Grace's cry was different this time, it was a lot more aggressive and deeper. Robbie could feel her hurt through the sound of her cry and the tremble of her body as she exhaled all of her emotions. He'd learned that a strong woman will do everything in her power to hold what hurts the most in but eventually the time came to let it all go. Grace had been through so much in her life with men and it never worked out, so she felt like a failure and like she'd continually let her children down. If anyone could understand Grace at this moment it was Robbie, they had been through hell and back together, she knew that no matter what decisions she had made, good or bad, he would be there for her no matter what. He was upset with Grace periodically because of her bad decisions concerning the men that she brought into their lives, but it never changed the way he loved her. Grace was human, and humans make mistakes. It was tough to see Grace in so much pain, and Anthony wasn't worthy of this sort of heartache. She knew she deserved better, but she was so tired of hopping in and out of relationships that when she met Anthony she decided that he was as good of a man as she could get.

Robbie knew that Grace needed him to be there for her and not criticize the mistakes she had made in life. He put his hand around Grace's shoulder and said, "Mama it's ok to cry, I know it's hard for you and it's hard for me to see you cry but I understand mama." She looked up at him, wiped her face with her hands and said, "Baby your mama hurt so much, and she is so tired, I know you understand because you love me, and you pay attention to me in every way and I want to tell you that I am sorry for putting ya'll in so much mess son. Ya'll don't deserve it and I hate that I did this to ya'll and myself again." Robbie kissed her on the cheek and said, "It's not your fault mama, some men are just bad men and you are too good for bad men, you just needed to go through all the bad ones to get to a good one. Mama you are going to have a good man one day so don't cry." She wiped her face again, stared at Robbie for a moment then replied, "You know I love you so much right?" He replied, "Yes ma'am and I love you too mama." She said, "I know you do and thank you for making his night. You really believe that I am going to find a good man?" Robbie said, "Yes ma'am, and you are going to be so happy too mama, he is going to spoil you like you spoil us!" She was smiling super hard and said, "Well how about this, you will be mama's good little man until the right good man comes along ok?" He smiled and said, "Mama I like that, and I am going to spoil you and when I get rich I am going to spoil you some more!" He was glad to finally get Grace to stop crying and start thinking positive, he knew that that's exactly what she needed to hear.

Grace was gorgeous, and she had such an amazing heart and will to love with everything inside of her, men took her love for granted and they

139

took advantage of her. Robbie hated that, and he wanted to hurt every man that had ever hurt her. Once it seemed like her spirits had been lifted Robbie asked, "Mama can we finish cleaning your room the way we always do with music?" She thought about it a minute and replied, "Yes son but we have to turn the music down low, so we won't wake up your sisters and brother. We have to clean up fast because it is getting late, you have to go to school and mama has to go to work." Robbie was so happy to hear Grace say that they could have this moment because he loved seeing her happy and enjoying herself, he replied, "Yes, ma'am I understand." It was time to get down just the two of them. Grace went and brought her record player into her room, plugged it in and told him to close the door. She was going through her records to see what song she wanted to play and finally she found 'The Isley Brothers' album, her favorite. She looked over at Robbie, smiled and put it on.

CHAPTER 25

The sounds were groovy and Robbie loved it, they were cleaning up and singing along with the music. Robbie watched Grace dance, smiling, and enjoying herself, music allowed her let go and be herself. It helped her forget about how cruel the world was. All of the stress, and negativity melted away with the music and she was able to escape to another world where she had no worries, and no regrets. This meant the world to Robbie, it taught him that no matter what was going on in his life, good or bad, he could always turn to music and allow it to take him away. Grace's room wasn't messy so there wasn't much to clean up. Robbie knew he didn't have much time left so he had to get his dance in with Grace, this was tradition, this was the icing on the cake, nothing else mattered. When they danced it felt like Robbie was giving Grace the respect, love, honesty, trust, happiness, and joy that she'd never had. Dancing with Grace was magical, it always made them both happy because it was a way to share their love as mother and son. Robbie walked up to her and said, "Mama, can we dance like we always do?" She smiled and replied back, "Son now you know that your mama was not about to let her baby go without their dance now come on and let's get funky!" He was ecstatic, it was time to get down with the get down and groove to the sounds of Earth Wind and Fire (Let's Groove) and it was on! They were doing their dance like always, he was holding Grace's hand and they jammed to the music, having an amazing time. Grace was smiling, clapping, rocking, and jumping while Robbie was making up his own moves. He did everything he could to try to impress her and she loved to watch him dance.

Robbie imagined that she was releasing all of her frustrations and anger while enjoying this moment. Things felt different though, as if they both needed to be in the moment, it reminded him of his dreams. Robbie paused, thinking that he had heard something, and he told Grace, so she turned the music down, walked into the living room and there was nothing. Robbie felt as if there was someone else in the house watching them, but

Grace had checked and there was nothing, so they continued dancing. He was still worried but tried to get back into dancing, Grace knew that he was feeling anxious, so she grabbed his hand pulled him closer saying, "Son stop worrying there is nothing out there I already checked." Robbie replied, "Ok mama." He finally stopped thinking about Anthony, he didn't want to mess up the moment because she deserved to finally be free and enjoy herself. She was so happy, and this was one of the best moments that they'd had in so long. Robbie tried to switch his thinking to good thoughts, he thought about the fun that their family would have now that Anthony was out of the picture. He imagined outings, shopping, tv nights, with no arguing, abuse or negativity and a smile spread across his face. When Grace noticed it, she said, "Aw, my handsome little baby look at that smile are you happy?" Robbie was blushing so hard that his cheeks were hurting, he looked up at Grace and said, "Yes ma'am." She smiled and said, "I am happy too and I am so sorry that I put my babies through this mess with that man." Robbie hugged her and rested his head on her stomach as they children danced and replied, "It's ok mama, people make mistakes you are not perfect and we all forgive you, I am glad that he is gone, and I hope that he never comes back." She replied, "Don't worry son he is never coming back I promise, he has hurt us all enough and I can't have a man around my kids that doesn't want to be a part of their life." Robbie was so happy to hear this, it made him feel good to know that she finally got the message he'd tried to send her indirectly, for years.

Grace had an amazing personality and was really funny, she knew how to make anyone laugh and have a great time, so she started dancing really funny doing some crazy chicken dance. Robbie was laughing so hard that he could barely breathe. Then he started imitating her and doing the same dance and she was laughing too. They were having such a great time dancing and laughing then all of a sudden, the door slammed open and smashed into the dresser, making everything fall on the floor. They children both jumped, and looked over to see Anthony standing there, eyes red, breathing hard and smelling like he'd bathed in alcohol! Robbie's heart felt like it had dropped to the floor, he didn't know what to do. This was his nightmare coming true! He knew he'd heard someone inside the house, so he had to have been inside for a while, stalking them.

Grace stood in front of Robbie, looked at Anthony and said, "Now I told you not to come back to my house unannounced!" Before she could get out the rest of what she was about to say, he cut her off and screamed, "I don't give a fuck what you told me bitch! I still got his stuff in here and I can come inside this motherfucking house anytime I get ready!" Robbie was fuming, he had called Grace out her name! He wasn't afraid of Anthony and this time he felt like he had to stand up to him once and for all! Robbie got in front of Grace, pointed at him and screamed, "Don't you call my mama a bitch, you a bitch I hate you!" Robbie knew that would piss him off, but he didn't care, he was ready to die for Grace. Anthony took his hand, hit it downwards extremely hard and said, "Nigga who the fuck you think you talking to don't you ever talk to me like that I am the fucking king I raised you motherfucker!" Grace jumped over Robbie and slapped Anthony so hard that he fell back towards the dresser then she screamed, "Don't you ever put your motherfucking hands on my child again, I will kill your ass I am not playing!" Anthony was stunned by how hard Grace had hit him and once he snapped back into reality he jumped up and grabbed Grace by the neck and she grabbed him by his neck. They were wrestling back and forth trying to see who could overpower who.

Anthony was on top of Grace choking her and Robbie was not about to let him hurt her, so he jump on Anthony's back and started biting him on his cheek! He jumped up started screaming as he tried to throw him off of, but he fell, and his head hit the closet door. Robbie still had not let go, he had a grip on Anthony's cheek as his head put a hole through the closet door. Anthony was very drunk because Robbie could taste and smell the alcohol on his skin. Grace was gasping for air trying to get focused, so it was Robbie and Anthony going at then he finally threw Robbie in the closet and put a chair in front of it, so he couldn't get out. Robbie was afraid for Grace and his siblings because of how often Anthony had told him that he would kill them all and I was locked in the closet and wouldn't be able to help. Robbie screamed for Grace to get up, he could see out of the closet from the little hole that he had put in the door with his head. Anthony headed towards Grace as soon as he'd locked Robbie in the closet, Robbie kept screaming "Mama! Get up Mama! He is going to kill you!" Grace was slowly getting up and she felt him grab her leg, as she crawled towards the door when Anthony reached for the hammer that had fallen on the floor by the dresser! Robbie began to panic because he knew that

Anthony would beat her to death with it. Anthony was so drunk that he couldn't focus so he swung to hit her and missed. Robbie was beating the door, crying, doing everything that he could to get out of that closet, but he was trapped. Anthony swung the hammer at Grace and missed again, saying, "I heard you and your spoiled, faggot ass son! He just want you to himself! Ya'll in here having a good time talking shit about me, always dancing and shit! I hate that shit! You didn't have to dance with his ass you need to dance with me bitch!" Grace was startled and still trying to get away, but she was exhausted from him choking her. Since he'd been drinking, Anthony couldn't feel anything. Grace screamed, "You are a crazy motherfucker! I am going to call the police on your ass!" Anthony replied, "Bitch I been crazy, you just finding that out! Call the police all of ya'll will be dead by the time they get here! We all will die one big happy family!" Robbie was still trying to get out of the closet, the other children must have been hiding he knew that they had to have heard what was going on.

Grace seemed to get a burst of energy and she reached to pull his hand from her leg, suddenly he swung the hammer and hit her on the top of her head! Robbie was hysterical, he screamed, "No Mama! Get off my mama! I hate you bitch! I am going to kill you bitch! Mama!" Anthony looked back and threw the hammer at the closet saying, "Nigga shut the fuck up you are next!" Robbie didn't see Grace anywhere after he had hit her, he wondered if she was still on the floor, but he didn't see her anywhere. Anthony stood up and staggered left to right, then he said, "Where are you bitch, get back in here and obey me or I am going to kill your fucking spoiled ass son!" Robbie was screaming, "Kill me! I don't care Kill me!" Anthony began walking towards the closet, Robbie was preparing himself to die but he didn't care because he'd hoped that Grace would take his siblings and get to safety. While Anthony made his way towards the closet, Robbie saw him stop and turn around slowly, and as he did that, Grace appeared. She was standing there with her shot gun pointed at Anthony. Grace pointed the shot gun at his chest and said, "I told you never to put your motherfucking hands on me or I was going to kill you!" Anthony started laughing as if what Grace said was a joke then he walked up and aimed the shotgun towards his forehead saying, "You are not going to do shit to me, go ahead bitch shoot me, pull the fucking trigger!" He pressed the gun to his head telling Grace to shoot him, clearly believing that she wouldn't.

She stood, staring at him with blood running down her head and then suddenly, she cocked the gun, and took two steps back. Robbie was terrified, he put his hands over his eyes and peaked through the cracks of his fingers. As Grace stepped back, Anthony stepped towards her and said, "You are worthless, you talked all of that shit and didn't do a motherfucking thing because you ain't no killer! You ain't shit! I am the king and you need to understand that shit once and for all! Take your ass over there and sit down after you apologize to me!" Robbie was in shock, he couldn't believe that Anthony was talking to Grace this way as she stood with a gun pointed at him. As Grace continued to stand there, tears rolled down her face. Robbie was beginning to think she might not shoot him after all, maybe she just loved him too much. Robbie put his head down and started to cry. Then Grace began to move, she was slowly switching sides with Anthony, maneuvering him away from the closet door, then she turned to look at Robbie. He had never seen this look before, he saw death in Grace's eyes. At that moment, he knew that life would change forever. Anthony looked at Grace, frowned his face and said, "What in the hell are you doing? Didn't I tell you to sit your ass on the bed and think about everything I said to you? Don't make be bust your ass again I am tired of you disobeying me!"

Grace took two more steps back, she looked at Robbie again and said, "It's going to be ok baby, everything is going to be ok I promise." Anthony started yelling, "Bitch stop talking to that gay ass son of yours before I whoop his little whining ass again!" Her eyes snapped back to Anthony, she put the gun to his face and said, "Before you what? You won't lay another motherfucking hand on my child ever again I promise you that!" Anthony replied, "I told you that the next time you put a motherfucking gun to my head you better use it and you better kill me bitch!" Grace took another step back, looked at Anthony and said, "Ok!" And she pulled the trigger as Robbie jumped back further into the closet.

CHAPTER
26

Robbie could not believe what had just happened, it felt unreal, Grace had killed Anthony and he'd hit the floor with a thud. There was blood everywhere, like something from a movie. Anthony was laying on the ground in a puddle of blood and there was smoke coming from his head. Robbie was in full panic mode, it wasn't supposed to happen this way. Grace was standing over Anthony's body crying, she got down on her knees, and started punching at his body screaming, "I hate you! I told you not to fucking touch me now look what you made me do! Look what you made me do to you!" Robbie was begging Grace to let him get out of the closet, so I could comfort her.

Finally, she let Robbie out of the closet and he slowly walked up to Anthony's body. As he got closer, he was able to see exactly where the smoke was coming from. Robbie looked at Grace, wide eyed and said, "Mama he smoking!" She replied, "Boy go to your room right now!" He took off towards the room and as he got closer, he saw his siblings standing by the kitchen crying and looking startled. Robbie didn't know what to do, his nerves were messed up. Jake was hiding, and the girls were trembling with fear. Robbie told them to go to their rooms because they did not want to see what was in Grace's room. Laura looked at Robbie and whispered, "Did mama shoot Anthony?" He replied, "Yes and he is dead." They took off running to get back in bed.

Grace was still in her room, but she had gotten very quiet, Robbie was afraid to go in and check on her because he didn't want to upset her even more. After all this time, the abuse, the hate that Robbie had for him, he'd wanted Anthony dead but didn't expect it to happen this way. He couldn't wrap his head around this scenario, it was too much to take in and it dawned on him that things were going to get worse from there. She had killed a man and would probably be going to jail. He thought about what would happen them and who would care for them if not Grace. He knew about foster homes and adoption, all outcomes that he'd never wanted for himself and his siblings. This was all happening because Anthony couldn't accept that he was no longer a part of their family.

Robbie getting angrier and angrier because he knew that their lives would be a million times worse without Grace. He hated that this had to have happened this way and was wondering what would come next. Grace began to cry again, and but he was still scared to go and check on her. She had killed the man she was madly in love with in front of her son. Robbie made the decision to call out for her, if she got mad he didn't care but he needed to make sure she was alright. Robbie screamed for her, "Mama! Mama! Are you ok!" She replied, "Don't come in here, I am ok, do not come in here!" Robbie said, "Ok mama." This was a disaster. All he'd ever wanted was for Grace and them to live happily ever after and now it didn't possible. Grace would be arrested, and they might get split up into foster homes.

Grace had committed murder. The thought if it made him shudder. Robbie's heart was beating so fast he thought he would pass out. He paced back and forth, waiting to hear from Grace again but all he could hear was his siblings whispering to each other about what had happened. They didn't have the image of Anthony laying in Grace's room with his head blown off, all they heard was the gunshot. Robbie thought to himself, "You will be ok, mother will be ok, nothing is going to happen to her, be calm God will fix everything just wait!" It sounded like the right thing to be thinking at that time but deep down inside he knew that something awful was going to happen.

Robbie looked out to see Grace walk out of her room, standing by the bedroom door with the telephone in her hand, she was looking down the hall at her children, the look she had on her face, they'd never forget. It was as if she knew she was about to lose them. She kept repeating the words, "I'm sorry my babies, I am so sorry." The children all stood by the door asking, "Mama what's wrong? Mama are you ok? Mama can we see?" Robbie was the only one that knew what had happened, the other children knew not to go where Grace was, but they were worried. Suddenly the phone rang, and she went out the front door to sit on the porch. She answered the phone, and broke down crying saying, "Please come and get my kids, I don't want nobody to take them from me sis!" She was talking to her sister about taking them so that they wouldn't be put in the system. When Robbie saw Grace break down like this, it shattered his heart because he knew that she loved them so much that in all this chaos she wanted to make sure they'd be ok. When she hung the phone up, she pulled out a cigarette, lit it and began to smoke. This was something Robbie had never seen Grace do, she didn't normally smoke but he understood why she felt like she needed to. She looked down at the phone, picked it up and started dialing again as Robbie wondered who she was calling next. He got his answer as she spoke and said, "I need someone to come to my house immediately, he put his hands on me and my child, so I killed his ass!" After hearing that Robbie knew that it was the police department that she had called. It was time to get everything in order because he knew that once the police arrived, things would go from bad to worse. Robbie noticed his siblings still sitting with looks of terror frozen on their faces, he told them to all get some of their belongings packed.

Robbie knew he needed to get his mind right. Grace walked back in the house, came straight to the boys' room, looked at him and said, "Listen son, I need you to be strong for mama, I need you to take care of your brother and sisters, I don't know what's going to happen, but I may be going away for a while and I want ya'll to stick together. Your auntie is on her way to get ya'll." Robbie was in tears, this was not what he'd wanted to hear but he knew what was coming, he replied "Ok mama." She called the rest of the children into the room and she told them the same thing. They were all crying at this point, it was one of the saddest moments of their lives. Robbie had never cried so much in his life, knowing that there was a possibility that they might lose her for life. Grace was holding them all tightly, when they heard the door open, and then a loud scream, it was Grace's sister, Aunt Cora she had rushed in and saw Anthony's body lying there. She started crying and said, "Girl what have you done? Why did you kill this man? Oh lord!" She repeated this over and over again, Grace left the children in the room and headed to where she was standing.

Grace stood at the door and turned to Aunt Cora saying, "I am sorry, he was trying to kill me and my kids, so I had to do it sis, I had to do it!" Aunt Cora started hugging Grace, looked at them and then said, "I will take the kids if anything happens, but you are going to be alright baby girl." The children were lost, they didn't know what to do, everything had happened so quickly that they were just standing there trying to take it all in. Robbie had butterflies in his stomach, he was trembling, and shaking because the time had come. The police sirens blared outside the front of the house as they pulled up, it sounded like the whole military was out there. Aunt Cora ran back where the children were and told them to close their eyes and follow her. Grace was standing at the front door waiting to talk to the police. As the children walked to the door where Grace was they heard the police through the loud speaker saying, "Please come outside with your hands in the air!" Grace put her hands in the air and began to walk outside, she looked back at them and said, "I love ya'll my babies!" Then she turned around and kept walking towards the yard.

The children all broke down into tears, the police stormed into the house and told the children to go out the back door with their aunt. There were police everywhere by the time they all made it outside. They all just wanted to know was where Grace was, Aunt Cora told them that their mother was fine she was just talking to the police. There were neighbors coming out from every house to see what was happening. The children were all put into a car to wait for someone to come back for them. Robbie could see Grace in hand cuffs talking to the police and gesturing towards them. The children were all going crazy inside of the car screaming, "Mama! I want my mama!" Robbie told them all to be quiet and that it was going to be alright but they were not listening. Finally, the detective who was talking to Grace came over to the car, opened the door and said, "Did any of you see what happened in the house?" They were all confused about whether or not they should say anything because they children didn't want to get Grace in trouble. The detective looked at them as if he knew that the children had something to say so he pointed at Robbie and said, "What's your name son?" Robbie just responded saying, "Why do you want to know my name? My mother told us not to talk to strangers sir."

He grinned and replied, "I see that you are a very smart young man, your mother was right you should never talk to strangers, but I am trying to help your mother out so if you know or saw anything can you please tell me what you happened?" Robbie didn't say a word, then the detective smiled and said, "Ok son if I get your mother and she tells you to talk to me, will you tell me something?" Robbie looked at him and then looked at his siblings and replied, "Yes sir, I guess." He walked back over to the car to get Grace and he brought her back to where the children were. He told Grace, "Ma'am I am really trying to make sense of this all and I know that the kids were in the house, so can you please talk to your son and tell him to let me know what he saw?"

Grace nodded her head then looked at Robbie saying, "Baby tell him everything that you saw for mommy ok, it's going to be alright I promise." Robbie was skeptical, he didn't trust the detective, but his mother wanted him to tell what happened, so he would. He frowned and said, "Ok mama." Robbie began to tell the story from beginning to end everything that happened, but the detective kept interrupting his story, asking him questions to try to switch up what he was saying. This made Robbie so mad that he stopped talking so they put them in back in the car and took Grace away back to the other patrol car. The other children kept asking Robbie what was going to happen to Grace and he just responded that they would need to wait and see. Grace was sitting in the police car looking at them as if she knew that she was about to go away for a long time. Robbie wouldn't have wished that feeling on anybody, not even his worst enemy except for Anthony! He was dead, and Robbie was glad that he'd died, he didn't deserve to live. He actually wanted to hit Anthony's corpse a few more times before they took it to the morgue. From day one that man had shattered their family, and now the children had to pay the ultimate price. He was dead, but the children were about to lose their mother because of him. Robbie sat, thinking to himself, "What are we going to do? Where are we going to go?" he was trying to prepare himself for the worst, he definitely didn't want to be separated from his siblings. Then he thought about the fact that he could end up in an even worse situation than I had already survived. And what if his siblings ended up being abused? Aunt Cora had kids of her own, so he didn't know if she would be able to take all of them. She was already doing her own thing, living her life, partying, and enjoying life so why would she want to stop all of that and take them in?

All Robbie had was questions and more questions. As they sat in the police car it felt like everything was moving in slow motion, he wanted to be with Grace, but the officers would not let them be with her. Robbie felt helpless, he couldn't protect Grace. All kinds of thoughts were going through his head, and he blamed himself for everything. If he had told Grace what Anthony had been doing a long time ago, they would not have been in this situation. But Robbie had done what he thought was best at the time. Suddenly there was screaming coming from the opposite side of the car, Robbie looked around to see who it was and it was his other Aunt, April. She was trying to get to Grace and yelling at the police officers because they would not let her speak to Grace. Then she came to where the children were in the car, she opened the door, looked at them and said, "I am sorry babies, everything is going to be ok, we will get your mother out of this mess." She hugged them all and then walked back to where Grace was, which was where Aunt Cora was also standing. They were talking to each other and looking back at the children. Robbie had already figured out what was about to happen, the aunts were going to split the children up. They'd take two a piece so that neither of them would be stuck with four extra kids. Robbie didn't want to be taken away from his siblings, but he felt some relief that they would all be with family members instead of with strangers who might them through hell again.

After what seemed like forever, the police, the aunts and Grace, who was being escorted by an officer, all headed over to the children and asked them to get out of the car. They all jumped out and ran to Grace to hug her as tight as they could. She asked the officer if he could un-cuff her so that she could hug them back and he took them off. Aunt Cora and Aunt April stood crying as they watched Grace hug her children with everything inside her. Grace looked at them all and said, "Listen to me, I want ya'll to go and stay with your aunties until I get back ok?" They were all crying and didn't want to agree with what Grace was saying but they replied, "Ok mama." She kissed each of them on the forehead, took a step back and said, "I don't know what's going to happen to me, but I want ya'll to know that your mama is not a bad person, I protected ya'll and I would do it again over and over for my babies. I want ya'll to be good while I am handling this, the boys will go together, and the girls will go together but ya'll will all be back together again ok? I love ya'll my babies!" Robbie felt so sick to his stomach knowing that she was not going to be back any time soon, but all he could do was hope and pray for the best. The children were being split up which meant that the boys would not see their sisters for a while. When the officers put the hand cuffs back on Grace and took her back to the car, the children began to scream and cry for her so Robbie did his best to try to calm them all down. He told them not to worry because everything would be alright, mama would be back soon. They finally calmed down and the boys and girls said goodbye to each other. They kissed and hugged each other as Robbie promised them that they would come to see them as much as possible if their Aunties would allow them to. Their whole lives, all they'd had was each other and they didn't know how to function being separated from each other and their mother. It would take some getting used to, but Robbie was optimistic that everything would be ok in the long run. He told himself that God allows things to happen for a reason. He had prayed for Anthony to be gone and God took him away forever. He was thankful for that prayer being answered.

In Robbie's mind, Anthony had been the devil himself, the way he treated him, beat and tortured him, he'd never forget. Robbie never did tell Grace or anyone else about the things that Anthony had done to him. He decided that he wouldn't speak about it until he was able to heal from it all. Despite the trauma he endured, Robbie saw his story as a victory because he'd survived and overcome so much. When he thought about what Grace would have to endure from that point on, he was even more thankful that they'd all survived. And as Robbie reflected on how things had reached that point he was still able to smile through his tears while thinking of that last dance with his mother.

CPSIA information can be obtained
at www.ICGtesting.com
Printed in the USA
BVHW031700180123
656549BV00001B/10

9 781728 305189